Beneath the Crust of Culture

Contemporary Psychoanalytic Studies
1

Beneath the Crust of Culture

Psychoanalytic Anthropology and the Cultural Unconscious in American Life

Howard F. Stein

Rodopi

Amsterdam - New York, NY 2004

Cover Design: Paul Pollmann

The paper on which this book is printed meets the requirements of 'ISO 9706: 1994, Information and documentation - Paper for documents - Requirements for permanence'.

ISBN: 90-420-0818-0

Printed in The Netherlands

To Melford E. Spiro, a scholar's scholar,
With gratitude

Contents

Foreword

The function of metaphor serves an exalted human dynamic: it communicates multiple, overdetermined meanings and desires while remaining a universal instantiation reflective of our shared humanity. In this highly illuminating and evocative book, Howard F. Stein is preoccupied with metaphor and meaning, imago and repetition, surface and depth—the process and transmogrification of culture. In our contemporary climate of uncertainty, volatility, rupture, and hate, Stein engagingly and cogently uncovers an array of recent events in American society that are both timely and of immense value for psychoanalysis today. Highlighting the unconscious edifice of American culture, the reader is invited to examine the deep emotional significance and unconscious resonance of terror, trauma, death, deracination, and the primordial anxiety that envelopes us all.

Investigating recent historical events that have ripped through American life and gripped world attention—from terrorism to school shootings and state execution—Stein demonstrates how destruction saturates the human psyche materialized in social defense, symbolic representation, and malevolent action. Beginning with the terrorist attack on the World Trade Center, the reader is plummeted into the horror, hysteria, and mass paranoia of confronting the motives behind that event, thus mobilizing indignation, hate, and free-floating anxiety in response to fear of persecution by fanaticism and foreign opposition. Exploring the politicalization of nationalism, religion, ethnic injustice, and economic exploitation leading to Third World envy, resentment, and retaliation, Stein explores the unconscious dynamics that kindle and sustain clashes between civilizations and antithetical worldviews.

Murder is a ubiquitous and uniquely human phenomenon. From the Columbine High School massacre to the execution of Timothy McVeigh, Stein argues that violence among youth is both a symptom and a metaphor for alienation and rage against displacement and disposability by antiseptic corporate culture. Stein delicately examines the pathology of identity, which in part is forged by our narcissistic victories, vulnerabilities, and shame, thus leading to redemption through murder. Taken to extremes, lack of recognition can lead from turning against peers to one's country—our paternal government, which is merely one appearance among many forms of devaluation of humanness by consumerism in workplace America. The clear implication of this book is that we groom our monsters, our enemies—enemies we cultivate, whom then turn on us through retaliation, which in turn we need to repudiate, terminate, purge from our consciousness, then forget. But this leaves a gaping wound in the collective psyche, which mobilizes the threat of anticipatory persecution and predation projected onto the foreign—the Other—fueling hypernationalism and xenophobia, a rigid identification with collective group narcissism based on a simple economy of similarity and difference. What happens when collective narcissism is besieged by natural disasters, bombings, mass shootings, and military defeats thereby leading to cultural helplessness, loss, and bereavement? It is here that Stein brilliantly advances an anthropology of mourning and society.

Taken together, these studies deeply engage the questions of victimization and trauma, displacement and emotional pain, social valuation and prejudice, intolerance to difference, and the unconscious identifications and fantasies that lie beneath the crust of culture condoning annihilation and murder under the guise of heaven, nation, and justice. This work is an extremely thoughtful, scholarly, and perspicacious foray into the human soul wielding profound implications for public and national policy from one of the leading psychoanalytic anthropologists of our time.

Jon Mills
Editor
Contemporary Psychoanalytic Studies

Preface

Things are not what they seem. Things are not what we want them to "seem." Things are not as we perceive and need them to be. This is true not only individually, but also when we are in groups called cultures. That is the theme of this book. It is a theme that will pervade and be illustrated by numerous variations drawn from contemporary American society. A psychoanalytic anthropological approach will be used to reveal the cultural unconscious in the American life of the late 20th and early 21st centuries.

Anthropologists have long spoken metaphorically of "the cake of custom." Presumably there is a recipe and a baker—or many. The organizing metaphor of this book, by contrast, is that of cultural "crust" and that which lies or even lurks beneath the crust. I do not propose a simple static opposition of, say, core and crust, or of filling and crust. Rather, I look dynamically—including psychodynamically—at the work of culture, at the dialectical (Ogden, 1989, 1996) relation between core and crust. The old volcanistic metaphor is especially apt: a thick, hard crust of earth, beneath which bubbles hot, liquid magma pressing for release above. The more recent image of tectonic plates moving and clashing beneath the seemingly uneventful surface is an equally compelling metaphor. Now, I will be the first to admit that cultures and their people are not crusts, cores, volcanoes, or tectonic plates. Rather, I argue that these images are fruitful guiding metaphors to understanding the nature, function, and process of culture.

One means of exploring the relation between what is on the surface and what is beneath is to carefully study cultural change—often catastrophic change—which is abundant in the United States and worldwide. Such a study takes one to the core of cultural processes, a core that is often at variance with the thick, encrusted surface images, pronouncements, agendas, self-presentations, and justifications. Most of the studies (chapters) in this book explore often-dramatic culture change in order to help illumine what culture is about and how it "works" (and fails to work). The links between chapters are less specifically substantive as they are methodological and theoretical. In each chapter, the surface picture or "crust" serves as the point of departure for the study of the dynamics of cultural complexity.

I do not apologize for the obvious fact that a study such as this "falls between the cracks" of many disciplines: among them, anthropology, sociology, group psychology, political psychology, psychohistory, and psychoanalysis. The data, the raw materials, of this study lead me more to the interstitial spaces between academic boundaries than to the spaces within a single discipline. I invite the reader on a journey, which, if successful, both subsumes and transcends professional boundaries. I have long felt that fidelity to the data—and to the people behind it—is far more important than protecting academic "turf." Or, to put it another way, this book aspires to an anthropology in its widest—and original—compass.

Through a series of studies, this book carefully "maps" the relationship between the official, espoused, often enforced picture of culture, and the deeper, often contradictory, underlying unconscious dynamics that link surface and interior. A psychodynamic perspective will broaden and deepen cultural analysis, and thereby reveal the unconscious foundation of much of American culture. Far from claiming that only local cultural studies are possible and legitimate (the post-modern position), I shall suggest that the local can help illumine universal processes in the not-always-wise human animal. This book builds on a number of my previous cultural studies, including *Developmental Time, Cultural Space* (1987), *Maps from the Mind* (1989), *The Culture of Oklahoma* (1993a), *The Dream of Culture* (1994a), *Listening Deeply* (1994a), *Prairie Voices* (1996a), *Euphemism, Spin, and the Crisis of Organizational Life* (1998a), and *Nothing Personal, Just Business: A Guided Journey into Organizational Darkness* (2001a).

Throughout my career as a clinical teacher of medical students, interns and residents, I have often received puzzled looks at my attempt to teach about the elusiveness of cultural interpretation and explanation. One story, however, that usually makes intuitive sense to them is when I tell them that my modus operandi is really the same as that of the popular radio journalist Paul Harvey. He begins by giving the conventional account of a news story. He then finds much information that contradicts the conventional wisdom and proposes a different version of the story. He always ends with the phrase: "And now you know the rest of the story." Now, I know full well that no individual or group story is ever complete or finished. But Harvey's approach has a ring of truth, and, as metaphor, becomes a link of understanding and empathy between my students and me. In exploring the relationship between the crust and what is beneath it, I hope to bring to the surface at least more of the story. If I accomplish this, I will have fulfilled my aim in this book.

One of Sigmund Freud's signal contributions to understanding people was the discovery (a) that the mind—thinking—is filled with conflict, (b) that we often defend ourselves from forbidden, anxiety-evoking, emotion-laden thoughts, and (c) that the thoughts we have are often compromise formations, that is, syntheses of disguise and revelation, secrecy and exposure, disavowal and discharge. We humans try to think and to not think something, to feel and to not feel something, at the same time. Anxiety becomes a central driving force in the organization of thinking and feeling, both individually and in the life of groups. The unconscious presses thought and feeling "upward" toward consciousness, but in a form where anxiety is minimized and pleasure is enhanced. The conscious form or representation of thought disguises the original thought.

Through displacement and condensation, the original emotion-laden thought or fantasy is subject to a myriad of distortions and masks that mystify and redirect the original, and give rise to metaphor, metonymy, synecdoche, and other "figures of speech" that leap from signifier to signifier, and simultaneously partially reveal and partially conceal the elusive object of signification. No wonder so much of human culture consists of a dense "forest of symbols" (Victor Turner's felicitous concept, 1970) and is lived in a conscious dream-like state (La Barre, 1972; Stein, 1994b).

The method of inquiry that will be used in this book is nicely described by Jerry Piven (2002) in his description of the method of psychoanalysis:

> Psychoanalysis is more than just an uncovering. It is more than simply assuming that what is manifest covers the latent content, as though one were just expecting the repressed to be lurking underneath the floorboards cozily. The unconscious is rather engaging in a process of elusion, and leaves false tracks, dead ends, mirages, seductive diversions. The psyche is that complex and cannot be predicted so easily. (p. 8)

Why are we so devious with ourselves? What have come to be identified as many "defense mechanisms" (A. Freud, 1936) serve as a means of protecting us from anxiety—often only to give rise to thoughts, fantasies, and situations that produce even greater anxiety, and that require additional bastions of defense. We ensnare ourselves in traps of our own making (see Devereux, 1967, 1980; La Barre, 1972). These defensive processes give rise to countless symbols and rituals—not only private but public, collective. We act as if the "crust" protects us from the frightening "core."

In this book, I build upon Sigmund Freud's (and his successors') approach to understanding human symbol and action (Freud, 1900/1953; Ogden, 1989, 1996), for understanding what people do individually and in groups (Freud, 1921/1955). Although this book makes a "substantive" contribution to the study of American culture, its more intended contribution is methodological, namely, the use of psychoanalytic inquiry as an exploratory instrument for cultural interpretation and explanation.

I shall not try to directly defend this proposition here in the Preface. Rather, I shall illustrate its utility as an interpretive tool throughout the case studies in this book. Explanatory power is the ultimate test of any explanatory scheme. Each study will explore the relationship between the declared, often official surface picture, and the hidden, often disavowed picture. Taken together, the studies will provide both argument for and illustration of the fruitfulness of the psychodynamic approach to understanding and explaining much of American culture and its recent history.

The first chapter examines the eventfulness of September 11, 2001 from the viewpoint of depth psychology. The second chapter explores the meanings and roots of the shootings at Columbine High School on April 20, 1999. The third chapter considers the execution of Timothy McVeigh in 2001 as a nodal cultural event. The fourth chapter examines hypernationalism and xenophobia, and explores their presence in the seemingly unlikeliest of all places—the American workplace. The fifth chapter discusses the Worcester, Massachusetts, fire of December 3, 1999, and in the light of the comparative study of disaster. The sixth chapter recognizes mourning to be a central process in every society, not only with respect to individual loss, but also with respect to threats to the group, itself.

Acknowledgments

My gratitude goes to Ms. Denise A. Deal, Ms. Stacy D. Wigley, Ms. Barbara A. Lightfoot, and Mr. Donald L. Clothier for their computer assistance—and their monumental patience with me — as I prepared this manuscript for publication. My wife, Nance K. Cunningham, lived through the evolution of this book and edited the final manuscript. I am indebted to her diligence.

Chapter 1 [Days of Awe] An earlier version of this chapter was presented at the annual conference of the High Plains Society for Applied Anthropology, Estes Park, Colorado, 21 April 2002, and published in the *Journal for the Psychoanalysis of Culture and Society,* 8(2) Fall 2003: 187-199. I am especially grateful to Dr. Mark Bracher and Dr. Deward Walker for their encouragement on this essay.

Chapter 2 [Disposable Youth] I wish to thank Dr. Mark Bracher for his encouragement and editorial assistance in this essay—in particular for the metaphor of the outwardly proceeding "concentric circles" as a principle of organization. Some editors inspire at least as much as they police. I wish also to thank Ms. Katie Farmer for her uncanny wizardry on the Internet in pursuit of substantive material on the Columbine High School massacre, and for her critique of my ideas. An earlier version of this chapter was published in the *Journal for the Psychoanalysis of Culture and Society*, 5(2), Fall 2000: 217-236.

Chapter 3 [Execution of Timothy McVeigh] An earlier version of this chapter was published in *Clio's Psyche*, 8(2), September 2001, 70-74.

Chapter 4 [Hypernationalism and Xenophobia] An earlier version of this chapter was published in "Hypernationalism and Xenophobia: A Thirty Year Retrospective," *Mind and Human Interaction*, 10(2), Fall 1999, 124-140.

Chapter 5 [The Left Out and the Forgotten] is based on a Keynote Presentation, "Catastrophe: Community Impact and Healing," Worcester Institute on Loss and Trauma, sponsored by University of Massachusetts Medical School and Youth Opportunities Upheld, Inc., Worcester, MA, 20 October 2000. The presentation owes much to conversations with Marjorie Cahn, Ed.D., the Worcester conference planning committee, Fred B. Jordan, M.D., Allene Jackson, M.D., John Tassey, Ph.D., and Cynthia Calloway, M.Ed. I dedicate this chapter to the memory of L. Bryce Boyer, M.D., eminent psychiatrist, psychoanalyst, and friend, who died 8 August 2000. An earlier version of this chapter was published in the *High Plains Applied Anthropologist*, 21(1), Spring 2001, 1-24.

Chapter 6 [Mourning and Society] An early version of this chapter was originally presented at a May 25, 2001 Conference entitled "Identity, Mourning, and Psychopolitical Processes," a conference hosted by the Center for the Study of Mind and Human Interaction, University of Virginia School of Medicine, Charlottesville. An earlier version of this chapter was published in *Mind and Human Interaction*, 12(2), 2001, 82-94.

One

Days of Awe

September 11, 2001 and its Cultural Psychodynamics

Near the end of September 2001, my then seven-year-old son Zev came home from school with, among other papers, a pencil drawing he had made. Everyone in the second grade class had been asked to draw something about Halloween. His was a simple sketch. In the center of the 8.5 x 11 inch sheet of paper was a tall, thin rectangular boxy figure, flanked on either side by a couple of long, concave, petal-like strokes. I asked him what it was about—was there a story? He said, "It's a haunted tower, and at the bottom is the haunted basement." I did not ask him for the geographical reference or for an interpretation. Nor did I think I needed to.

Together with his parents, he had watched with horror the televised events of September 11, 2001, unfold in New York City, Washington, D.C., and outside Pittsburgh. We were all struggling to find some form with which to represent what happened. This chapter is no different. It is an attempt to comprehend, from many viewpoints, the days of awe that began on September 11, 2001, and which persist to this day. It is about how cultures often come to be haunted by calamities that befall them. And it is about the psychoanalytic interpretation of culture as a tool for unmasking the cultural unconscious. We, who think we must struggle hard to find "psychoanalytic data" about culture, really do not have to work so very hard. These data are readily there—painfully and liberatingly there. This chapter begins with a cataclysmic event, traces out the cultural meanings and feelings built up around the event, and explores meanings and emotions behind the event.

Many understandings of and explanations for the September 11, 2001, jumbojet attacks on the World Trade Center and Pentagon were offered in the immediate aftermath of the event. This chapter offers a psychoanalytic perspective on the event and on cultural/ historical accounts of it. Specifically, the role of irrational factors, their symbols and political actions, are explored. The events of September 11 resulted not only in immense destruction and loss of life, but in an assault on the American cultural sense of self and of group boundaries. In this chapter the attacks are interpreted psychodynamically with respect to the symbolisms of place, and with respect to the larger cultural sense of place and of history among Americans and among those who attacked America—and those who supported the attacks.

The attacks resulted in a sense of violation and humiliation, in the experience of narcissistic injury, and in the effort, through war, to reverse that experience and restore group pride. At the same time, the terrorists and other radicalized Muslims were recoiling from narcissistic injury from the West as well. I argue that, in part, September 11 is the expression of a "crisis cult" of modernization and globalization (Devereux, 1955; La Barre, 1972) among many Islamic peoples, and that it in turn triggered a "crisis cult" (going to war) in the United States—first the war with Afghanistan, later the war with Iraq. Through an exploration of the symbolisms of September 11, 2001, and of the response to the attacks, I offer a preliminary interpretation of the meanings and causes of the attacks, and of the response to the attacks.

INTRODUCTION

I approach with humility the task of offering a preliminary psychological understanding of the causes and meanings (Spiro, 1986, 2001) of the September 11th attacks on the World Trade Center in New York City, and the Pentagon in Washington, D.C. The world was abuzz with instant—and repeated—replay and almost immediate analysis. The task of sorting through the cultural rubble is neither easy nor quickly done. The sorting becomes all the more difficult when one takes into account the American penchant for assigning blame as the predominant mode of explaining risk and disaster (Douglas and Wildavsky, 1982; Douglas, 1992). Although I shall discuss many themes from September 11, perhaps the overarching theme is that of boundaries: their permeability, their violation, their collapse, their reaffirmation—Americans', the attackers', those who identified and urged on the terrorists, and so on. It will be my thesis that "Political beliefs and the real world actions that follow from them … are fed by irrational motives" (D. Lotto, personal communication, February 1, 2002). At the same time, this thesis points to a complexity of the social world that cannot be reduced to a simple, straightforward account. I wish it were otherwise.

LANGUAGE AND QUICK CERTAINTIES

Words are commitments. Description, narrative, interpretation, implications, conclusions—none is without a prior commitment, usually unstated. Of the September 11, 2001, attacks upon the World Trade Center and the Pentagon, so much has already been written. Policy has been made; action has been taken. Initial confusion and bewilderment quickly gave way to certainty and to military action ("Either you're with us, or you're against us."). The pressure for knowing and acting was both confounded and made more urgent by the fact that the enemy could not be defined or confined geographically. Part of the terror of terrorism is the free-floating anxiety, if not panic, it induces. To a degree the anxiety was contained by the American government and media's quick focus on Osama Bin Laden, the al-Qaeda network, and the Taliban government of Afghanistan as the enemy in "the new war."

What began as sheer horror has been thoroughly conventionalized, beliefs about it stylized, and its implications are the doctrines of opposing camps. One side of the conflict grieves, another side cheers. Both sides wage war against the other. Accounts congeal within a matter of a few days. What is there left to say that does not trivialize or sentimentalize? Should it not be difficult to say something that can encompass the scale of the assault and the catastrophe? Even trauma-language can be a flight from what occurred and continues to occur. Trauma-language can serve primarily as a defense against anxiety while seeming to be an accurate depiction of reality and our emotional response to it. Our words bear the responsibility for the emotional work they might haltingly do—for ourselves and for others. This fact is the only ground that overcomes my own hesitation to speak about the unspeakable.

There has been much official talk about closure, about rebuilding, about resilience, about returning to normal or creating "a new normal" (a term that originated after the 1995 Oklahoma City bombing). My own starting place is shards, broken vessels, the sense of brokenness, itself. My feeling parallels the images I see: the desecrated, later consecrated "Ground Zero," the twisted metal and rubble and mass grave of the Twin Towers of the World Trade Center; the smashed-in Pentagon; and the heroically crashed jet in western Pennsylvania. There is too much to understand—too much to ingest, swallow, digest, and metabolize in a short time.

On the morning of September 11, 2001, hardly had two hijacked jumbo jets been flown into the World Trade Center Twin Towers, and one hijacked jumbo jet into the Pentagon, than a torrent of words rushed in to fill the void, to contain the terror, and offer meaning to what had just happened. Through language people attempted to wrest some control out of the incinerating inferno. Language, in turn, offers a key to underlying fantasies upon which action became based. In the United States, and among its allies, old and new, the weeks that followed saw stories elaborated, and from them, preparation for action: e.g., "Pearl Harbor all over again"; "Freedom has been violated"; "Ground Zero" (the site of the attacks, initially desecrated, now a sacred place, named for the sites of the first atomic bombs); "911" (the date of the attack [9/11/2001] conflated with the emergency phone number); "It happened here"; "Freedom has been violated"; "a different world after September 11"; "America will never again be the same"; "America is brought to its knees—in prayer"; "American crusade"; "democracy and freedom versus fanaticism and terrorism."

DISASTER AND MEANING

Just as people make meaning of disasters, they also bring meaning to disasters (see Stein, 2001b). We not only create meaning afterwards, but, at least to some extent, we "know" the meaning beforehand. What *is* occurs as it *should*, according to fantasy and its cultural representation. Reality serves as embodiment and repository of unconscious wish. Here, projection is anticipation, and reality is confirmation. David Levine pithily notes: "we cannot allow anything we do not already know to exist (and we are supposedly the children of the modern world)" (personal communication, March 17, 2002). It is as if we are unconsciously poised to give form to events before they occur. Events follow story lines and become woven into them. If the September 11th attack was itself a thrust by terrorists into the United States, so too were the American accounts impositions (projections) upon the event. Many antecedents were held to explain the calamity: ranging from Charles Martel's victory in the Battle of Tours at Poitiers in 732 and Jan Sobieski's victory in the Battle of Vienna in 1683 (both, decisive battles at the boundary of Islam and Christianity), to Islam's expulsion from Andalusia (al-Andalus) in the 15th century, to American abandonment of Afghanistan in 1989 and American policy toward Israel. Narratives of American audacity and exploitation vied with narratives of Third World envy and resentment. Secular modernism was pitted against religious fundamentalism. American self-blame vacillated with protests of innocence and recrimination.

Three popular cultural texts articulated much of the national discourse: Samuel Huntington's *The Clash of Civilizations and the Remaking of World Order* (1998), Bernard Lewis's *What Went Wrong: Western Impact and Middle Eastern Response* (2001), and Benjamin Barber's *Jihad vs. McWorld: How Globalism and Tribalism are Reshaping the World* (1996). Huntington's thesis is that future violent conflicts will be based on religious and ethnic ideologies rather than economic or political ones. His idea is not new (see, for instance, *Idols of the Tribe: Group Identity and Political Change*, by Harold R. Isaacs, 1975/1989). The White Ethnic Movement of the late 1960's and 1970's in the United States (Stein and Hill, 1977) was built on ethnic ideology. For another thing, the Marxist political-economic ideology that fueled the Russian Revolution and the subsequent Soviet Union was in large measure a reaction against the Orthodox Church-dominated Tsar. Further, at a deeper level, the ostensibly economic-political ideology drew much of its psychological inspiration from mystical Russian collectivist thought (Mueller, 1957). Finally, a wide array of ideologies can serve similar underlying unconscious (irrational) motivations. What seems at first glance as a clash of civilizations can be seen as more specifically as a clash of wounded collective narcissisms, Islamic and American. I shall discuss this below.

Lewis offers a sweeping view of Islamic culture and history, describing it as a religious-political mindset in a way that is akin to the earlier more static studies of national character. He describes Islam's cultural decline from the fifteenth century, a reversal that took place after widespread leadership. His interpretation of Islamic history suffers from being unilateralist and not, at least in part, a product of interaction with the West. His image of Islamic civilization is more monolithic than is often the case—similar to many earlier views of socialism and communism. He thus sees the current expressions of Islamic violence and revitalization as more a natural outgrowth than as a "crisis cult" (La Barre, 1972) of that history. There is room, I believe, in Lewis' argument for an examination of people's feeling (affect) about their own cultural decline when they compare themselves to the West, as well as the fact of that decline.

By contrast with Huntington and Lewis, Barber's essay is a deeply interactionist one. He sees the contemporary world as built around the colliding polar opposite forces of "Jihad" (meaning reactive religious dogmatism and tribalism) and "McWorld" (meaning economic globalism and consumerism). In Barber's view, European colonialism and American capitalism (in the form of transnational corporations and communication networks) in part provoke ethnic and fundamentalist protest in the form of terror and other mass violence. Intrusive "McWorld" induces a defensively reactive "Jihad." Barber sees "McWorld" not only as a threat abroad, but also as a serious threat to democracy. His interactive view leaves room for one to interpret narcissistic vulnerability in many Islamic peoples at the hands of transnational economics—and resurgent narcissism to wrest victory from defeat and to return their culture to a pristine past. Barber oversimplifies, though, the role of the U.S. and the West, who are not only hegemonic villains and exploiters, but also liberators. America as symbol and presence, is at once lure, hope, oppressor, and betrayer. Modernity not only does things to people, but for them. Often, people seek what liberations modernity offers, only to be frightened, guilty, and ashamed for it (Stein and Hill, 1977).

Taken together, Huntington, Lewis, and Barber and their books can be seen not only as scholars and scholarly treatises, but also as cynosures, whose narratives fulfill latent national discourses. It is as if there are inchoate narratives that precede events, poised to claim and to fill them with (projective) meaning. And behind these narratives lie what Lloyd deMause (1982) calls group fantasies of unconscious motive, desire, and defense—that is to say, shared unconscious fantasies that underpin culture. George Devereux (1956/1969) wrote that much of cultural folklore is held in emotional "cold storage" until emotionally needed, whereupon belief becomes direct experience. When the attacks in New York City and Washington, D.C., happened, we—whoever constituted the "we" worldwide—already "knew" much of what they signified. In the United States, from a summer of 2001 filled with news stories and cartoons of shark attacks upon innocent swimmers, to the popularity of computer flight-simulating video games featuring attacks upon skyscrapers, and movies about terrorist attacks upon America, imminent danger was in the air. The popular 2001 movie *Pearl Harbor* was still in active memory. Its role can be likened to *China Syndrome* in 1978, six months or so before the Three Mile Island disaster in 1979. But, then, taken superficially, sharks were just sharks, and computer games and movies were only entertainment. What at one level was already known in fantasy, at another level constituted a devastating "surprise attack" upon unsuspecting innocence. Surely the course of response and recovery from trauma becomes complicated when there is unconscious collusion with its occurrence.

Put differently, mass trauma is often partly the result of the courting, tempting, and provoking of reality. Culture always anticipates and rehearses for later reality, even for reality for which its members consciously feel unprepared. When the heroic firefighters planted the American flag in the rubble of the World Trade Center, one immediately "knew"—recognized via projection—that a re-enactment of the Asian Theatre in World War II was taking place. These firefighters were immediately likened to the marines who raised the American flag on Mt. Suribachi, Iwo Jima, on February 23, 1945. Past was merged with present. Idealization of "The Greatest Generation" was followed by merger with it—and with the sacrifice it required.

In early November 2001, film director Robert Altman argued that the then-current wave of violent movies had "created the atmosphere" that "set the pattern" in which terrorists' thinking and acting out mass destruction could thrive. I am arguing for neither causation nor correlation, but instead for the same kind of tacit cultural suggestibility that occurred when a spate of gun-cartoons and gun imagery on magazine covers preceded the assassination attempt on President Ronald Reagan (deMause, 1984). The analysis of cultural fantasy helps to disclose cultural and historical motivation. Just as we live in the aftermath of the recent popular movie *Pearl Harbor*, we also live in the aftermath of an event that was immediately likened to Pearl Harbor—and in the shadow of a longing for the togetherness and purposefulness that supposedly characterized the American people during World War II.

In a review of the spate of American war movies in late winter 2002, Chris Vognar writes:

> Given the standard Hollywood production schedule, the current war-movie craze has more to do with a four-year-old film than current events. Steven Spielberg's *Saving Private Ryan* [1998] wasn't just a great movie: it was also a cultural touchstone for the country's revived interest in World War II—the setting for both *Hart's War* and the recent *Dark Blue World*. Along with Tom Brokaw's book *The Greatest Generation* and the HBO miniseries *Band of Brothers*, Ryan made war movies noble again (after a long, skeptical series of Vietnam films). (2002, p. 6J)

To these must now be added *Behind Enemy Lines*, *Black Hawk Down*, and *We Were Soldiers*, movies released in early 2002. Still, to say that *Saving Private Ryan* explains the genre of movies that followed it, requires further explanation in terms of the cultural timeliness of the group fantasy it expressed, fulfilled, and sustained. An even earlier film is also part of the national drama: *Titanic*, released in 1997, was a partly fictionalized account of the audacious launching, reckless driving, and sinking of the "unsinkable" luxury liner in 1912 (Batteau, 2001). For all the world, the Titanic might be thought of as a metaphor for modern America. With the events of September 11th, the U.S. suffered "narcissistic injury to our [grandiose] fantasies of invulnerability [and fueled] our need to seek vengeance and humiliate our 'enemies'" (D. Lotto, personal communication, February 13, 2002). Many Americans hoped that, through war, the sense of shame associated with the "success" of the September 11th assault might be undone.

THE NEED AND SEARCH FOR ENEMIES

For the U.S., the decade after the collapse of the Soviet Union and the end of the Cold War had been filled with a search for a sustainable, good-enough enemy: Japan, Iraq, and China none of which attained this permanent status. The "War Against Terrorism," with its promise to be long-waged, was as much a solution to the problem of chronic, diffuse anxiety as it was a problem to those who also—and consciously—sought solid, safe borders. A decade of unfulfilled search gave way to the identification of an external enemy—one who had for the first time in American history since the War of 1812 managed to penetrate American continental boundaries. At last, Americans could hope again to discriminate between "us" and "them," the good and the evil, respectively. So could those who visited the terror upon the United States.

In the years prior to September 11, the American Ghost Dance had already begun. From the viewpoint of the unconscious, the September 11 attack ended the search for a reliable enemy upon which to externalize, and which could contain, repudiated American "badness" (e.g., aggression, ambivalence over freedom). David Levering Lewis (2002, p. 40) writes that "before September 11, the Bush administration had announced an end to American observance of the ABM Treaty, committed itself to a quixotic Maginot line in space, dismissed the environmental goals of Kyoto, and gone out of its way to find reasons not to attend the Durban conference on racism." In a similar vein, Carlo Rotella observes that "Compared to most of those with whom we share the planet, Americans (including those who have reason to regard themselves as unlucky or oppressed) lead a collective life of fabulously let-them-eat-cake profligacy" (2002, p. 49-50). He continues with the observation that, "in our popular fantasies,"

> We have been rehearsing the events of September 11... quintessentially in the action movies that have perfected the formula of explosions, collapsing buildings, malign perpetrators, and special-effects bystanders sent pinwheeling by gouts of orange flame. The action movies of the 1980's and 1990's stink of hubris and ingratitude; in retrospect, they seem to suggest that a whole culture was asking for it (which is not the same thing as deserving it when it happens. (p. 50).

Later: "We were always in harm's way; the bad news was always coming; we should have been more engaged, less thoughtless, more vigilant, less satisfied" (2002, p. 51). "Innocence" was more cultural protest than self-evident fact. Recklessly, we Americans were going to do things our way. Projecting our inner struggles with our own aggression onto the cinema screen, we still lacked a well defined enemy. It would quickly coalesce on September 11.

Almost immediately after the attacks on the World Trade Center and the Pentagon, "Islamic terrorists," and then Osama Bin Laden, the Al-Qaeda network, and the Afghanistan Taliban leadership (and later still, President Saddam Hussein of Iraq) became the overdetermined focus of evil. Terrible as the attacks were, they symbolically, if only partially, resolved the decade-old problem of intense, free-floating anxiety among Americans. The U.S. had found a group through which anxiety could be at least partially contained. Cokie and Steven Roberts (2002) wrote:

> The old ideological struggle between East and West is being replaced by a cultural and religious conflict between the Judeo-Christian and Muslim worlds. A new Berlin Wall is going up, but it is a mental barrier, not a physical one. It is a wall of hostility and misunderstanding, not concrete and barbed wire. (p. 27A)

In a "successful" war effort, "cold" or "hot," a group projects its bad parts and dreads into the enemy. After the attacks of September 11, the identification of the enemy—the boundary between "us" and "them"—was far from clear-cut. One can even speak of an unconscious cultural collusion between enemies. During the Soviet era, the U.S. had had its McCarthyist searches for and purges of "the [communist] enemy within" American borders. From the jet airline attacks on September 11, through the subsequent mailing of anthrax spores, it likewise became difficult to distinguish between "us" and "them" within American borders. At least during the Cold War there had been a vast geographical separation between the United States and the Soviet Union (and "Red" China). We were "here" and they were "there," far away from us. Furthermore, apart from spying and the chronic "Red Scare," there had been no evidence of physical penetration. September 11 changed that. "Over There" (the famous song of World War I, and the place where "The Yanks are coming") became "Over Here" as well. The battlefield, though, was not occupied by conventional soldiers, but rather by ordinary citizens and terrorists. And the place of battle consisted of highly symbolic charged workplaces: the World Trade Center was entirely civilian. Under such circumstances, it is especially difficult to get rid of—to contain outside—the free-floating anxiety over the location of terror, and of the war.

Further, United States did not mobilize ideologically or militarily after the then-recent bombings of the American embassies in Tanzania and Kenya. The "foreign" bombings did not carry the symbolic, emotional, significance of New York or Washington, D.C. They were outside the psychological membrane. The American embassy, though "ours," was "over there." Americans could still feel safe within in their psychogeographic boundaries. If with these national boundaries people feel secure, these boundaries also place people at risk for dangers that "cannot" happen within them. Permit me a tentative clinical formulation: the counterpart of terrorist paranoia was America's hysterical denial. I shall elaborate on this idea below.

From September 11, the relative psychological "comfort" the Cold War had provided was no longer possible. American public officials urged citizens to lead a normal, consumerist life while being vigilant for terrorists and acts of terror. Paradoxically, many Americans felt psychologically safer, even "invincible," under the threat of "mutual shared destruction" and "nuclear winter" than they currently do waiting for the next terrorist act to occur. Sadly and tragically, one "psychogeographic" legacy of the Cold War—heir to earlier attitudes of Manifest Destiny and isolationism—was to make an attack on the continental U.S. unthinkable, unimaginable. Here, as often occurs, cultural "defenses" in fact endanger their inhabitants. They help to create the permissive psychological climate that makes the unthinkable thinkable (to those who would attack the U.S.) and do-able. We not only need enemies (Volkan, 1988), but we also create enemies by provoking them. We and our enemies project aggression, provoke aggression, and then justify our own aggression as defense. In a world divided into true believers and infidels, David Levine (2002) writes of the fatal psychological symbiosis of faithful and infidel:

> When the unfaithful self is projected onto external objects, the aggression we attribute to it becomes their aggression directed at us, their desire to destroy our faith. We must now mobilize aggression to protect ourselves against the infidel, notwithstanding the fact that the threat he poses is the threat of connection with our own split off and disavowed faithless selves. Since the infidel's rejection of the good object is also our own, the aggression we attribute to him is also our own aggression outside and experienced as a threat to us. (p. 52)

The attacks on New York City and Washington, D.C., had the immediate effect of "healing"—at least temporarily—many splits within the U.S. Immediately after the April 19, 1995, bombing of the federal building in Oklahoma City, Oklahomans demonstrated to the nation and to the world the bountiful generosity of America's Heartland. Many Oklahomans proudly contrasted their local response with that in New York City after the 1993 bombing of the World Trade Center: the warmth of the American "center" differed from the coldness of the American "coasts." September 11, 2001 changed all this. In their abundant generosity, New Yorkers showed that the heartland could be present as much in that east coast city (supposedly too busy for heart) as anywhere.

A few days after the attacks, a newspaper cartoonist poignantly planted the American flag in place of the stem of a big apple. The metropolis once widely despised as impersonal and vile (akin to Fritz Lang's 1927 film *Metropolis*), was once again the idealized "Big Apple" of goodness, togetherness, and opportunity. If I may hyperbolize, Americans suddenly "became" New Yorkers, and New York became a symbol of American vulnerability and resilience. Only good was to be found in these spaces now. If even for a time, American psychogeography was now more united than split into good places and evil places. The us/them split came to be made between the American "sleeping giant" and the terrorist enemy.

In the days and weeks following the September 11 attacks, Americans and their elusive enemy were both equally regressed to their respective Dreamtimes. On the one hand, "the infidel" would be made to leave "the land of Muhammad (Saudi Arabia)"; on the other hand, "democracy" would be freed of the scourge of "terrorists." Each became "The Evil One" in mirror image to the other. Both, in fact, became "infidels" to the other's true belief.

DISASTER NARRATIVES AND FANTASY WORK

Homogenizing cultural narratives of the September 11 calamity are supposed to be experienced as the entire story. Such stories contain and enforce the cultural belief about what and who are significant and what and who are not. For instance, the official heroes of September 11 are the firefighters, the police, and the emergency medical personnel. The stories of some groups are newsworthy (group fantasy-worthy), and the stories of others are mostly omitted—for instance, the merchants of New York's Chinatown who were virtually blocked into isolation during the rescue; and the ironworkers in the long aftermath of the disaster, many of whom not only painstakingly dismantled the rubble of the World Trade Center, but who were the builders of the Twin Towers thirty years earlier (see Silver et al., 2002; Stein, 2001b).

The monumental architecture of midtown and downtown Manhattan could scarcely be fathomed by the miniaturization that television silently inflicts. Indeed, early viewers of the attacks on the buildings thought they were watching a science fiction movie. On the morning of September 11, as I stood watching the television monitor in my department's atrium, I experienced "narratives" differently from those being articulated by the popular media and the government. As I watched the countless replays of the second jet approaching and penetrating, then exploding, the South Tower, the attacks upon the Twin Towers felt to me like an immense rape scene: the two jets as vicious phallic thrusts piercing vulnerable tissue. Yet, the Twin Towers were themselves proud, audacious, American phallic thrusts into the technological New York City and American skyline. Symbolically, it felt as if the attacks (instruments of projective identifications) were intended to turn symbolic American "maleness" into "femaleness," and in turn to transform the feminized adversaries of America into potent, triumphant males. The collapse of both towers into a mass grave shows how far the symbolism of (national) castration or emasculation can go.

If the attacks upon the Twin Towers (economic supremacy) and the Pentagon (military supremacy) were attempts to symbolically castrate the "bad" American father in order to idealize the "good" Islamic father and deity, the attacks could also be construed as the terrorists' own self-castration of their own disavowed youthful oedipal strivings against their own fathers. Those who attacked the U.S. thus transformed themselves into obedient, "good," sons of their purified father and of Allah. In this image, America condensed as an image into the bad father and the disobedient son. This is to say that American unconsciously, symbolically became the repudiated "bad self" and "bad object" of the terrorists themselves.

The attacks and their symbolism tell us much about the terrorists and about those in whose behalf they acted—those for whom the terrorists were psychological proxies or delegates. The attacks in New York and Washington suggest an attempt at communication via action, that is, an attempt to transfer an unbearable emotional state, to be rid of it by literally injecting it into America. In part, Americans' reactions—induced emotions—can tell us further about the perpetrators' rage, humiliation, shame, and grief. In short, the events of September 11 can be subjected to the kind of symbolic analysis that adds a psychological dimension to the widely held contention that modernization and unchecked development engender anomie and social problems such as alcoholism, drug abuse, and divorce. For instance, consider the American name given to the initial phase of the 2003 war with Iraq: "Shock and Awe." Rudolph Binion writes: "That war was launched by an aerial attack on the nerve centers of Iraq's capital and main city: shades of 9/11. It bore the distinctly traumatic code name 'Shock and Awe'" (2003, p. 1). The shared American experience on the morning of September 11, 2001, was surely one of shock and awe.

In a similar vein, much has been written about "Why they [al-Qaeda, the Taliban of Afghanistan, and many Muslims in the Near and Far East] hate us." We can learn about the depths of this hate both by examining the castration symbolism described above and by examining Americans' emotional responses to the attacks. In part, we can study those who hate Americans by studying our own emotional response to their actions on us. Instead of trying to understand the emotional states, though, Americans are more likely to act on ("act out") them through war—to be rid of them, to deposit them back in the enemy, and to further engage the enemy. In the name of self-defense, escalation of conflict and further entanglement in it reduce the possibility of comprehension and de-escalation of conflict. Rudolph Binion (2003) writes that

> The haunting remembrance of 9/11, the memorialization and mourning, have hardly diminished since the event, which has meanwhile crept into the subsoil of our fantasies and nightmares. We have defended against its recurrence in its original form by focusing vital counterterrorist controls inordinately on airports and immigrants, as if bin Laden would simplemindedly try the very same stunt a second time. And we are conjuring up 9/11 in thin disguise through a war on Iraq which, billed as a war on terrorism,

> is as if calculated to promote more terrorism—a textbook case of traumatic reliving. (p. 1)

Such conscious strategies to avert past trauma in the future only serve unconsciously to provoke its repetition.

AMERICA AND THE SYMBOLISM OF NEW YORK CITY

Symbolically, America became both the site of the evil for the enemy, and the place where Americans struggled for a renewed sense of goodness. It seems as if part of the reaction to the shattering of the illusion of invincibility was an intense shame ("It couldn't [shouldn't] happen to us."), as if the successful penetration of the U.S. boundary was experienced as a humiliation. Part of the response, military and ideological, was a defense against the sense of shame. The sense of innocence and the assertion of pride can in part be traced to this defense.

It is little wonder that flag-displaying patriotism, decontamination efforts, and intense border vigilance (the Patriot Act, the new cabinet level Department of Homeland Security) are under way in the United States, since America (the idealized land of the good, bountiful mother) cannot altogether keep good in "here" and place bad out "there." The symbolism of New York City is a crucial part of the symbolic "healing" of America. New York City itself had long been a projective target within the United States, its image alternating between idealizing goodness and demonizing badness. The "Big Apple" (boundless opportunity, rebirth, immigrants' portal into the United States, "wholesome fun") has also at various times been the "Rotten Apple" (the alluring, sexy, defiling, destructive metropolis, the jungle). This ambivalence has been banished (repressed) since September 11. For a time, most Americans "became" New Yorkers—by identification, by a shared sense of vulnerability and by renewed resolve.

The cultural symbolism of New York City can be further illumined by examining the classic film *King Kong* (1933). For this, I draw on the insights of Kenneth Bernard. Emasculated, the ape-monster King Kong "seeks to attach another penis to himself" (Bernard, 1987, p. 126) in order to mate with Fay Wray. The Empire State Building becomes his prosthetic penis. "He will ram the Empire State [Building] into Fay as if it were (as in a sense it is) his very own" (1987, p.127). In the end, "For raising the specter of what has been so poignantly lost (and forgotten [repressed]), he must be viciously cut down. Civilization has too much riding on its Empire State to give it up" (1987, p.128). Technologized, mechanized, rationalized libido triumphs. "Beast that he was, he revealed the civilized man's flaw of too much thought and insufficient instinct" (Bernard, 1987, p. 46). Near the end, "When the planes come and shoot their tiny sperm bullets, it is not so much at Kong as at his penis, to the tip of which he has finally got Fay Wray. And when he lets go of it, he falls to his death. The penis is kept as a monument, hollowed out with offices and elevators, and called the Empire State Building. And New York is called the Empire State (the King Kong penis state: it is our answer to the jungle out of which Kong came)" (1987, p. 49).

In the least, then, the Empire State Building, and later the World Trade Center, represented if not also flaunted American technological prowess and economic potency to the nation and to the world—a thought that I hope will not be rejected as obscene in the face of the calamity. Just as New York City is a symbol to Americans, it is also a symbol to those who attacked America. On that fateful day, two symbolic audacities collided. I wonder: do the terrorists, and the peoples in whose behalf they act as emotional delegates, feel impotent, and project their impotence forceably into the United States? Is that, in part, what they are trying to "tell" America through their attack on the World Trade Center and the Pentagon? To gain "theirs" must they destroy "ours"? Is potency (personal, group) a zero-sum-game? The World Trade Center, and by extension New York City, became both a symbol and a trophy for those bent on destroying it and with it American morale. In short, both sides, then, felt assaulted, as much psychologically as physically, and needed to assault the other to recover.

THE COLLISION OF PAN-ISMS

The collision course of American and Radical Islamic cultures toward September 11, and the subsequent war in Afghanistan and Iraq, can be seen as examples of the fateful symbiosis of two "pan-ismic movements," contemporary Pan Islam and the congealing of militant nationalism in the United States. In pan-ismic movements historically, a natural affinity is "discovered" (while in fact an elective affinity is created, see Hobsbawm, 1983; Fallers, 1974) between erstwhile strangers and enemies. "Primordial" bonds (religious, ethnic, national) are not always ancient. Historical and contemporary social segmentation is dissolved and denied, at least ideologically, in the new collective. Differences are overcome in a harmonious unity in which all become siblings of one great extended family.

In a succinct formulation of the dynamics of pan-isms, Stephen Lukashevich (1968) writes:

> All Pan-isms, which sought union with one's racial brothers, were attempts at rolling back history to a common point of department. By the same token, all Pan-Isms repudiated as a historical mistake their dolorous national self-identity, which they wanted to replace with a new collective identity. In other words, all Pan-isms preached a collective rebirth. It can be said, therefore, if one would use a biological simile, that all Pan-isms, which promised national rebirth, had to start by returning to the womb together with all the tribes that sprang forth from it.... This neurotic aspect of Pan-isms played an undoubtedly important role in the formulation of Pan-ist ideologies.... (p. 121)

"All Pan-isms," he notes with a lengthy list, "have appeared in the wake of social or military catastrophes." Analyzing Polish Pan-Slavism, "which developed roughly between 1772 and 1830, in other words, from the first partition of Poland to the insurrection of 1830-31," he writes, "[it] was a wish to recreate 'regressively' a new Polish self-identity by losing the old one in the anonymity of Slavdom composed in its vast majority of Russians—hence their Russophilism" (1968, p. 121). The Pan-Slavists suffered the "devouring feeling of social inferiority" and "feeling of social insignificance" (1968, p. 121). For the Pan-Slavic Poles, Russia was the big brother, father, and mother who would protect the vulnerable Poles who suddenly felt small.

Lukashevich cautions against "an attempt at rationalizing an irrational situation" in the case of the Polish Pan-Slavists who are often seen with hindsight as traitors or as farsighted politicians for having been pro-Russian. The latter is irrelevant to the deep emotional structure of pan-isms which Lukashevich clarifies. Cultural rejuvenation, political organization, and social activism are all seen to flow from irrational premises based on regression. The biological simile is in fact a psychodynamic process by which the individual and the collective group attempt to regain the symbiotic tie to the idealized mother, to fuse in idealized organic oneness prior to differentiation from her (individuation).

Today, much as both Radical Islam and American nationalism have identifiable conscious "interests" and rational "agendas," these rest upon feelings of narcissistic vulnerability and injury, and on the attempt to repair if not undo the hurt by violent collective means—an undoing that only widens the vicious spiral of anxiety and defense (Devereux, 1955; La Barre, 1972). The oppositional creation of internal cultural sameness, fueled by regression, lies at the heart of all pan-isms.

CAUSALITY, SYMBOLISM, AND MEANING IN TERRORISM: MORE QUESTIONS

How shall we understand the cause(s) of Islamic terrorists', the Afghanistani Taliban's, and many Islamic people's hatred for the United States? What makes the U.S. so vile a country, one "deserving" brutal attack? The most common explanation among many Islamic peoples and many American intellectuals is (1) the exploitive, destructive, abandoning, foreign policy of the United States, coupled with (2) the catastrophic cultural consequences of modernization and economic globalization upon Islamic and other traditional peoples, including the destructive effect of the Internet. Part of this is American self-blame, and some is blame cast by those affected. Blaming "us" and blaming "them" are part of the poisonous projective process in need of further understanding. Demonization generates one type of explanation—but not the only one.

What can we glean about causality and meaning from the symbolism of the attacks and of the places chosen for attack? Jet planes pierce and explode gigantic phallic towers that are icons of a culture (America), of modernism and of globalization; likewise, they pierce and explode into that nation's military hub. What does the symbolic feminization of America signify in the unconscious of the attackers and those who support them?

What fantasies, wishes, and defenses might be carried out through the choice of these specific symbolic and ritual acts? Castration of Father-America? Projective self-castration of oedipal desires? For the sake of argument, consider the following: if the attacks are upon a bad father, what were the attackers' relationships with their own fathers and mothers, their childhoods, like? International relations and American exploitation seem to be necessary, but not sufficient, explanations for the hatred of the U.S. and the West. Might a reciprocal projective identification be taking place between Osama Bin Laden and the U.S. (personified in President George W. Bush) such that the U.S. unwittingly provokes and confirms externally Bin Laden's unconscious representation of the "bad father?" (The same may be asked of the relationship between President George W. Bush and Iraqi President Saddam Hussein.) Further, if self-destruction is the only path to heavenly paradise in Radical Islam, might the unconscious dynamic be the self-destruction of and purification from all flesh-borne desires, in order that one may at last be loveable by the (supernatural, ethereal, idealized) father? Do the United States and its embodiment of modernity represent the lures of the "flesh" and of separation-individuation from the mother-land and mother-religion? Where is the symbolically absent mother in this imagined drama? Taken to its extreme, in this apocalyptic patriarchal theology, the entire mother-earth may be renounced if not destroyed for the sake of ascent into father-sky. Such cultural dreams and imagery are not entirely foreign to the Christian doctrine of The Rapture.

Yet another level or dimension must be considered. Behind the public mask of patriarchy lies the mother. As Erik Erikson wrote, "Father religions have mother churches" (1958, p. 263). The prize for total self-surrender if not literal self-annihilation is not only love from the father, but reunion with the preambivalent mother. That is likely what the great cry for "unity" is about. Displaced oedipal triumph over the father—the "bad" father—is directed against foreign targets.

David Levine writes (personal communication, March 17, 2002): "consider the consequences of the oedipal defeat of the father and the construction of the father as ineffectual (a "paper tiger" to recall an older incarnation). Oedipal triumph over the father means that development is unnecessary and that the son can now imagine himself living forever in the primitive dyad with the mother," who is conspicuously absent in the official religious and national rhetoric and imagery. Levine wonders: "Could the prospect of oedipal triumph for the son have something to do with the failure to mourn (e.g., to mourn the loss of hope to retrieve the primitive dyad)?

Giving up the mother leads to maturation (development) just as triumphing over the father leads to regression." Both sides aspire to internal unity—Pan Islamic and American—a symbolized reunion with the idealized mother. Both sides, too, engage in an internal purification campaign to purge all badness and guilt. The "prize" for these regressive and otherwise defensive processes is possession of both (symbolized, idealized) mother and father, the obliteration of reality, and the killing of at least many thousands of people.

In the U.S., by symbolically "returning" in fantasy to the heroic, halcyon days of World War II, some may avert direct oedipal conflict with the father and its attendant guilt, by identifying with the stronger grandfather. Thus, by "becoming" the symbolic grandfather generation, oedipal triumph is achieved at home and abroad. One symbolically "resolves" oedipal ambition and guilt by leapfrogging over one's discounted, devalued father (after all, George Bush Sr. did not "finish the job" in Iraq, and the Bin Laden family "betrayed" Saudi Arabia and Islam) and glorifying one's stronger, "purer," grandfather's generation.

THE UNITED STATES AND RADICAL ISLAM AS REPRESENTATION

I am increasingly convinced less by broad explanations based exclusively on "what America did/does" to Islamic countries, or "what modernism/ globalization/poverty does" to Islamic countries, than by accounts that also examine what the United States *represents* and how people arrive at these specific representations. The U.S. became a "Satan" to Radical Islam, while, in his January 2002 State of the Union speech, American President George W. Bush spoke of an "Axis of Evil" that consisted of Iraq, Iran, and North Korea. The symbolic representation of the enemy as the personification of evil other does not happen via a simple stimulus-response psychology. In an insightful essay, "The Psyche of a Bin Laden," David Ignatius (2001, p. B7) argues that Bin Laden writes and sounds more like the Russian anarchists Prince Peter Kropotkin or Mikhail Bakunin than like an atavistic religious fanatic. I would add that Bin Laden's Pan Islamic romanticism sounds much like nineteenth century Slavophile Alexei Xomyakov's romanticist Pan Slavism (Stein, 1976)—or, to bring it closer to home, to the glorification of ethnicity and the vilification of American culture made by adherents of the New White Ethnic Movement in the United States of the 1960's and 1970's (Stein and Hill, 1977). Methodologically speaking, the dialectical tension between the intensive case study (local in space and time) and the comparative method bear much fruit in anthropological and broader social science understanding.

In a phrase, Bin Laden, like his counterparts in other times and places, sounds less like a self-assured "native" and more like a self-conscious "nativist." If Bin Laden and his Al-Qaeda compatriots are culturally like violent nativists of other places and times, then his hate is at least in part projected self-hate, resting upon guilt and shame from having been tempted by modernity and its places (America, Germany, France). Much of Bin Laden and associates' virulent hate derives at least in part from their having tasted, or being tempted by, liberation, that is, emotional separation from their native culture and its orthodox religion. The political reality of the perfidiousness of American foreign policy interacts with the intrapsychic experience of oppression by America, which is the projective expression of the wish to separate (Koenigsberg, 1975). The nativistic movement is at least in part fueled by the heroic, paranoid defense against that new identity. Just as modernization has many faces, so do terrorism, nativism, and the motives that drive it. For preliminary psychological sketches of the lives of Osama Bin Laden and Mohammad Atta, see Goertzel (2002), Kobrin (2002), and Immelman (2002).

One expression of the terrorists' defense is what George Devereux and Edwin M. Loeb (1943) termed "antagonistic acculturation," the use of an opponent's means to preserve or achieve traditional ends. Al-Qaeda know Western and modern ways because part of their psyche has become Westernized and modernized. Unconsciously, they embody the wishes they now consciously disavow. For instance, writer Phil Floyd (personal communication, October 28, 2001) observes that "Bin Laden is not a man with a simple martyr complex or who in any way is entertaining the idea of the 'ultimate sacrifice for Islam.' He is instead a very, very clever entrepreneur busy at personal myth building, consolidating power, and establishing in the hearts and minds of his followers visible hard targets." He knows the West and its modernism so well as to exploit it against itself. The West and its modernism have become internal as well as external presences.

In his *Washington Post* article, David Ignatius (2001) offers a thumbnail sketch of Muhammad Atta (apparently the coordinator of the attacks) that gives a psychodynamic dimension to the catastrophe. Far from being a traditional Islamic man, Atta is a member of the "disaffected elite." His life and end suggest a nostalgia for what he lost and to which he could never return, save through death:

> You could hardly find a more modern Arab than the suicide pilot Atta: He was raised to excel at engineering by an ambitious, overbearing father, and at the same time sheltered by a protective mother who bounded him on her knee until he went off to college. He eventually left Egypt to study in Germany, where he became lonely and embittered and fell into bin Laden's orbit. (p. B7)

In a similar vein, Winifried Kurth (2002) writes that

> Three of the suicide pilots have lived and studied in Hamburg—Muhammad Atta already since 1992. Later, while preparing the attacks, they lived in the U.S. and participated in everyday life. Osama bin Laden himself comes from an extraordinarily wealthy family with diverse connections to international business; the

> family—including OBL—had adapted a Western lifestyle already in the Seventies. (p. 125)

Observations such as these are promising to scholars, not only for the understanding of a single event and its subsequent history, but also for the comparative study of violent social movements as responses to many forms and ages of modernity, and for helping in policy formulation. For instance, Adam Goodheart (2002) begins with a quotation from Marshall Berman, and ends with a panorama of September 11.

> The cultural critic Marshall Berman, in selecting a title for his 1982 treatise on the experience of modernity, borrowed a newly resonant phrase from Karl Marx: All That Is Solid Melts Into Air. "To be modern," he wrote, "is to find ourselves in an environment that promises us adventure, power, joy, growth, transformation of ourselves and the world—and, at the same time, that threatens to destroy everything we have, everything we know, everything we are." It is to ride atop a skyscraper, to soar in an airplane. And both threatened us with such destruction, not just on that machine-bright morning in September, but long before. (p. 14)

CONCLUSIONS: GRIEF AND UNANSWERED QUESTIONS

I conclude mostly with questions—ones that might point us to unconventional answers, not only to understanding September 11, 2001, but to undertaking any psychoanalytic study of culture and society. So many questions remain unasked, and in turn unanswered, because they do not correspond to official and popular narrative accounts, and to the group fantasy and cultural mythology beneath them. If the al-Qaeda terrorists seek immortality through martyrdom, they do not do it alone. Is not some amount of provocation by the terrorists also involved, one that engages the United States (and its allies) via unconscious identification to play out the reciprocal role of counterplayer? And is there not reciprocal provocation by the United States?

If there is some historical truth to the accusation of American abandonment and exploitation of the Near East, does the U.S. not also play an unconscious and symbolic role (a Durkheimian "collective representation"), one which now generates and provokes its own reality? Put differently, what is the interplay between what we do to others and what we represent to others, between what we actually do (achieved status) and what we projectively are (ascribed status)? Do not cultures often "get what they unconsciously desire"—which often differs from conscious agendas and rational interests? Do not opposing groups "dance" in some kind of reciprocal unconscious adversary symbiosis (Stein, 1982a)? Further, can this dance with our enemies—who do bad things to us—be separated from the bad things we do within our own national group?

Such a split is common. In the Soviet Union, Stalin was a master of this displacement of his own terror onto the Nazi menace and the Great Patriotic War (World War II) against Fascism. Furthermore, do not the leaders and followers of currently warring groups have childhoods and families of origin, as well as political-economic realities, that affect decision-making? What do these warring groups represent to each other, and what are the overdetermined roots of these symbolisms? Finally, what good are borders (psychological, geographic) if they cannot keep their promises?

I leave this interpretive chapter and its subject with an overwhelming sense of incompleteness. I accept this void in knowing as necessary. Conventional and stylized accounts are at worst defenses against understanding the meaning of the attack, and at best they are partial truths. What we can know now is limited by the complicated process of mourning (Volkan, 1997; Stein, 2001c). Yet, it is often unbearable to mourn, so we flee into violent action.

As America focuses exclusively on "What they [the enemy] did and does to us," we have failed to pay attention to "What we Americans did and do to ourselves." Long before September 11, the decade-and-a-half long legacy of "managed social change" from downsizing and restructuring, to outsourcing and reengineering, have symbolically disposed of millions of Americans in the service of instant bottom-line inflation and a surge in shareholder value. The "Enron Scandal," in which company officials took millions of dollars from a collapsing corporation, while prohibiting workers from selling shares, thereby losing their entire retirement savings, emerged in early 2002 as internal American self-destructiveness on an unprecedented economic scale. What and who the United States becomes now as a culture, and what we do in the world, after September 11, 2001, rests upon what and who we value, and not only what and who we oppose.

There is so much more to be known and felt, beyond culturally stylized sentiment and sentimentality, ideologically right thinking, nationalistic jingoism, and obligatory action. People died on that terrible day because people could not be recognized as real people. They could only be recognized as symbols, embodiments, part objects. People were killed and people killed others because who and what they unconsciously represented consumed their existence as distinct, differentiated, and integrated persons. Many more will die, will be killed, in the name of heaven and nation. The psychoanalytic work of comprehending September 11, 2001, is scarcely begun.

From a cultural significance of September 11, 2001, I turn now to a study of the local and wider cultural significance of the Columbine High School shooting of April 20, 1999, in Littleton, Colorado. My approach to discovering a cultural unconscious will be the same as in a first study: carefully examining narratives, images, language, and metaphor to reveal more of "the rest of the story."

Two

Disposable Youth

The 1999 Columbine High School Massacre as American Metaphor

> "He was their son—but they didn't know the kid who did this," spoken by the minister who buried Dylan Klebold (quoted by Ellen Goodman, 1999, p. 1)

INTRODUCTION: THE CONCENTRIC CIRCLES OF A SCHOOL SHOOTING

This chapter attempts to address the questions: What does it mean to approach the April 20, 1999, massacre at Columbine High School as a cultural event? And what are the *unconscious* determinants, meanings, and ramifications of this event? I thus set for myself three inter-related tasks in this chapter: (1) an understanding of the massacre at Columbine High School in Littleton, Colorado, on April 20, 1999; (2) an understanding of physical violence (knives, guns, bombs) by adolescents in America; and (3) an understanding of the psychodynamics of American culture of which (1) and (2) are at once symptom and metaphor. I shall argue that the slaughter of youth by youth at that Colorado school is *in part* an extension of the rage against the imminent disposability felt by tens of millions of Americans in an increasingly corporate-dominated culture. In the process, I hope to illumine such behavioral science conundrums as: understanding human aggression, understanding contemporary "violence in the workplace" (a widespread social problem and category, see Allcorn, 1994), and understanding the relationship between perpetrators, victims, and bystanders (Hilberg, 1992)—a relationship that constitutes a single overarching culture.

This chapter will explore the very nature of psychodynamically informed cultural explanation for a catastrophe that has been exposed to universal gaze and interpretation by satellite-facilitated television. Specifically, how does one conceptually link large cultural processes (indeed, species-specific human biology) with local events? Specifically, how do social processes, structures, values, and change in the wider culture contribute to the triggering and later construction of such events as the Littleton, Colorado, high school massacre? Further, how do cultures (people in groups) explain "themselves" to "themselves?"

In summary, this study will attempt to bridge the exploration of a single catastrophic event with the larger epistemological issue of psychodynamically informed cultural explanation itself. Stated differently, it will address the interlinked questions of: What kind of *people* does this? What kind of *culture* does this happen in? What kind of *animal* (in the phylogenetic sense) does this? My working metaphor to organize this chapter is a kind of mental map, in which one proceeds outwardly from the center of a circle—the shooting itself—to further, more encompassing circles of understanding and explanation (an image I owe to Mark Bracher, personal communication, January 11, 2000).

Ever since Denver, Colorado, was selected as the site of the trial of Timothy McVeigh for the 1995 Oklahoma City bombing, many of my friends and colleagues in Colorado were uneasy over the fact that the trial would be held in the Federal Building in their state. Many who frequented or worked in the Denver Federal Building feared that it might be bombed. They were haunted by the prospect that what had happened "there" in Oklahoma might happen "here" in Colorado. Oklahoma, not Colorado, was the site of unheard-of violence. No doubt Freud's "narcissism of minor differences" (1930/1961) was part of the dread. Colorado shares part of its geographical and political border with Oklahoma. On April 20, 1999, "there" became "here," and the boundary contamination was fulfilled—just as on April 19, 1995, in Oklahoma City, and more broadly in the U.S.A., what could "only" happen in Beirut or Bosnia happened in the American "Heartland." A central part of the eventfulness of the Oklahoma City bombing, and of the Littleton high school massacre, was that the unimaginable became reality.

I approach the Columbine High School massacre as a cultural condensation, a symbolic convergence as in dream-work. I hope to account in part for the cultural configuration that includes: Black trench coats, guns, ambush, us/them, there/here, group polarization, Hitler's birthday, Aryan ideology, Gothic images, death-obsessed rock bands, violent video games (Doom, Duke Nuke 'Em), jocks (athletes), racism, adolescent cliques, guns, bullets, pipe bombs, arsenal, model families—"How could this have happened here?", disbelief-chagrin-outrage-grief.

All the natural sciences, social sciences, and humanities grapple with the question of "How do I know something?" This chapter, in the process of addressing this facet of countransference, likewise grapples with the question: "How do I *not* know something?" or "How do I go about *avoiding* knowing something?" Resistance to knowledge is part of knowledge. In a moving essay on "Psychoanalytic Listening to Historical Trauma," Dori Laub and Daniel Podell (1997) address the question of knowing and resistance to knowledge:

> [W]hat makes an entire nation resist the knowing of atrocities and become perpetrators or passive on-lookers to atrocities? Or, alternatively, what enables an individual, community, or nation to understand the significance of a historical trauma as it is occurring

> and to act on that knowledge. What are the variables involved in mediating the complex movement between the two poles of the continuum of knowing? (p. 259)

This chapter is a contribution to understanding the nature of cultural knowing, not-knowing, and what Bollas (1989) terms the "unthought known."

The material for the interpretations offered in this chapter on the cultural locus of the Columbine High School massacre is provided in the culture "itself" (if I many be allowed to reify group process for a moment, to make the point). The interpretation is already embedded in the folklore, in the language, in the best-selling business books (Freud & Oppenheim, 1958; Dundes, 1984). The psychodynamic interpretation about culture and symbolism is not some add on (Paul, 1980). It is a matter of seeing and hearing, of feeling, what is there. Countertransferentially speaking, one must, in fact, unconsciously try hard not to look, see, and feel.

One final preliminary thought: this chapter is, without *conscious* design, a sequel to a paper on downsizing and managed care (Stein, 1999a). Although I began research for, and writing of, this chapter with no prior thought of a connection, it soon emerged *from my unconscious*. One trusts the unconscious of the observer to reveal the unconscious at the heart of culture. Disposable *youth*, I have found, are inseparable from disposable—and disposed of—*adults*. The public *Kulturkampf* waged against the urban homeless is the most open expression of this disposal. If in the earlier piece I argued that unconsciously motivated political violence is rationalized as economic necessity, here I explore the shadow this casts into the next generation (see also Devereux, 1956, 1980).

CULTURAL NARRATIVE, CULTURAL UNDERSTANDING, AND THE COLUMBINE HIGH SCHOOL MASSACRE: FROM "LONE GUNMAN" TO "BAD SEED"

In this section I focus on the nature of explanation in American popular culture: that is, on how an "event" comes to be defined within the bounds of the paradigm. No sooner had the gunfire begun around 11:30 AM on April 20, 1999, at Columbine High School in Littleton, Colorado, than accounts of it began to emerge: from what happened to why it happened. Quickly, culturally saturated "narrative truth" merged with the "historic truth" (Spence, 1982) of the event and came to define it. It soon began to sound like other similar cultural stories in its cast and type of characters, sequence of events, story line, motivational inquiry (why the actors did what they did), the boundaries of the event (who was and was not on stage), and the like. The massacre became quickly woven into often-competing discourses, diagnoses, or interpretations: for instance, "parental responsibility," "the power of the peer group," "bad genes," and "vulnerable temperament."

Certain cultural categories quickly emerged as part of a recognizable taxonomy: violence, schools, teens, gangs, adolescence, workplace, safety, control. The Columbine shooting became part of standardized ways of accounting for the way events "like this" happen. The way they *do* happen becomes an extension of the way they *should* happen. That is, they come to conform to a largely projective cultural (group) aesthetic that becomes as coercive as any "art" form. Things do not merely happen: the ways they happen, and the reasons they happen, are as obligatory as religious rite. To inquire into, to question, the "logic" of the event is to open oneself to accusation of disloyalty, even harm. Part of the psychological function of the standardization of the account is to prevent anything vital from being missing; an equally vital part is to assure that any missing parts incompatible with the narrative (as defense) will be rejected.

It should be clear that we have entered the realm of a group's folklore about itself (La Barre, 1969, 1972), a folklore expressed in its official or popular "cultural psychology," what Erikson called its "actuality" (1964)—its social reality principle (in contrast with its underlying cultural psychology). In a different language, this is the "culturally constituted behavioral environment" (Hallowell, 1955) each group construes to be reality. A group's explicit cultural psychology is an extension of its ethnocentrism: as if to say, "The way we view the world is the world." It consists of a group's projective interpretation onto (into) itself and the world (social and natural) of how and why things happen. The popular cultural psychology articulates a society's folk science and folk (or popular) psychology. These latter, in turn, are elevated into official cultural doctrine and practice.

The purpose of cultural experts and their various "media" is to provide "facts" that will help corroborate the official cultural psychology and in turn "confirm" the prevailing folklore. A well-documented example of this process is that of alcoholism and drug abuse in the United States, wherein emphasis is placed on the independent agent and agency of "substance" to the neglect of its role as symbol (Fingarette, 1988; Heath, 1989; Stein, 1990a; Stein, 1993b).

A central tenet of United States' popular cultural psychology with respect to violence is its (if I may anthropomorphize culture for the sake of argument) insistence on a strictly individual psychology and responsibility as opposed to a group or cultural one underlying the event. Exceptions to this occur when the target or victim is a culture hero (e.g., John F. Kennedy, Martin Luther King, Jr.), in which case a "conspiracy theory" is more commonly invoked. For "ordinary" cultural atrocity, individual motivation, family history, "background check," "personality profiles," and the like constitute the search to explain why, when how, and by whom terrible things happen. The model used is often called the "lone gunman" or the "crazed worker" explanation. The causal, linear, thinking of popular culture assumes the narrative character of a "Who dunnit?" detective or gangster story or film:

there is a clearly demarcated villain (or pair, small group) who is held culpable, and who is to be found and brought to justice. Stylized and formulistic psychological and family-based explanations co-exist and contend with putatively biological accounts ("criminal gene," "bad seed").

This model not only directs cultural members *toward* certain explanations, but *away* from others–precisely those that would implicate the "normal" in the "abnormal" (Devereux, 1980). I have formulated this approach in earlier studies of American notions of alcoholism (Stein, 1982b, 1985, 1990a, 1993b). *Mystification is part of the very process of explication.* Not-knowing is central to knowing.

At stake is the nature of cultural understanding, including cultural self-understanding. The boundary of responsibility protects the larger group from being anything but victim of the process. The split, articulated in the boundary between "ordinary people" ("the good folks next door") and "monsters," must be preserved at all cost (see the *Time* magazine cover story, 3 May 1999, titled "THE MONSTERS NEXT DOOR": "the" and "next door" are in white, and "monsters" is in red).

What are "monsters" and "monstrosities" supposed to look like? Universally, "monsters" must look like "them," never like "us" (Malefijt, 1968; Stein and Niederland, 1989)—which fantasy makes the realities of the 1995 Oklahoma City bombing and the Littleton, Colorado, high school massacre even more disturbing, because at least in the "racial" or "ethnic" sense, "they" are "us." This boundary conflation in turn makes the quest for boundary-delineation even more urgent. Freud's "narcissism of minor differences" (1930) again here comes into play for major defensive purposes. Just as in the Oklahoma City bombing, so with the Littleton, Colorado, shooting, differences had to be created, since the "monsters" were not at all the classic image of *Homo monstrosus*.

They were not some living gargoyle, but appeared like the majority of "white folks." Adults had to engage in the same sort of "radical" distinctions we have come culturally to associate with the extremism of adolescent thinking. *Emotional distance* (the result of distancing) had to *create and widen* the gap formed by geographic, physiognomic, and cultural proximity and likeness. Further, it is to be remembered that the assailants—Eric, Dylan, and their fellow Trenchcoat Warriors—viewed the ostensible high school "normals" as monsters and monstrosities as well.

The media (television, radio, newspaper, magazine) serve a vital psychological role in interpreting an event in American culture to the culture in such a way as conventional defenses are affirmed. Ostensibly a source of disseminating information, the media present and re-present shared fantasy, wish, and defense. For something to be deemed "newsworthy" by the media, it must conform to unconscious fantasy and conscious folklore. Ironically, then, at the unconscious level, new but emotionally captivating "news" is already known.

Psychohistorian David R. Beisel (1999) describes how his university classroom discussions on the day following the Columbine shootings "echoed discussions in the media" (1999, p. 58). The unsaid and the culturally unsayable are the underside of the said and the sayable. It is almost as if the media provide the "secondary elaboration" rather than the "dream work" itself—yet claim to present the dream itself, and are believed. Beisel writes:

> …the media not only provides information, but also performs a defensive function. It is as if the media is an analysand, presenting all kinds of detailed data while hiding impulses, fantasies, and wishes through denials, rationalizations, displacements, projections, and the avoidance of facts (or topics) that might hint at the truth. (1999, p. .58).

Where, at this early stage Beisel asks, were inquiries about the childhoods of Klebold and Harris, and comparisons with accounts of the early lives of others who commit atrocities. The preservation of not-knowing is one of the psychological functions of cultural knowing, media-supplied and otherwise.

In its issue of December 20, 1999, *Time* devoted much space to disclosing, describing, and attempting to interpret the five secret home made videotapes that Klebold and Harris made to "tell why they did it" (Gibbs and Roche, 1999, p. 40-59). The essay provided much additional information, some of which I shall draw upon in this chapter. But it also serves as a kind of subsequent "secondary elaboration" to the prior cultural wide-awake "dream," and as a kind of re-working and up-dating of a folk-tale: to provide more "data" while preserving the defensive structure and function of the narrative.

We learn from "The Columbine Tapes," for example, that on what they called "Judgment Day," Harris and Klebold had hoped to kill 250 people, a slaughter that did not limit itself to specific categories of people against whom they would avenge themselves. We learn that "the assault did not go as the killers had planned. They had wanted to bomb first, then shoot. So they planted three sets of bombs…. [one, set a few miles away, as a lure for the police; another in the cafeteria, to drive terrified students into the parking lot, where Harris and Klebold would wait to shoot them; and a third in their cars, timed to explode when rescue workers and police arrived]. What actually happened instead was mainly an improvisation" (Gibbs and Roche 1999, p. 47). We learn that when Klebold found Cassie Bernall, "he leaned down. 'Peekaboo,' he said, and killed her" (1999, p. 48); that Harris and Klebold not only staged the massacre, but rehearsed it, saw it in the idiom of drama, and imagined movie directors Steven Spielberg and Quentin Tarantino fighting over their story (1999, p. 42). Others quickly interpreted Harris and Klebold as seeking martyrdom, fame, and immortality.

For the psychodynamically oriented theorist and culture critic, more remains unsaid than said with the revelation of the videotapes: For example, why the child's game, "Peekaboo," in an act of terror? Might the enactment of being seen, ridicule, exposure, shame, and rage have some place in understanding the deadly re-play—and the planned-for scale of the slaughter? If a kind of obliteration was at least planned, what are the roots of the need for such colossal destruction? The latest answers that we are offered are treated by the media as end-points rather than as way stations, as facts, rather than as metaphors. I intend to revisit these issues in more detail later in this chapter.

In the United States, we conceptualize and explain violence in terms of certain social "units"—units that one may readily infer from scholarly, popular, and media accounts alike. We look for the "smoking gun." Even popular psychobiographical accounts look for Newtonian-like cause-and-effect. From recent school and workplace shootings, to the 1986 U.S. Post Office massacre in Edmond, Oklahoma, the widespread American myth of the "lone wolf," the "lone madman," or the "crazed (individual) worker" unconsciously obscures the psychological overdeterminism that affects the "choice" of who the assailant(s) will be, and how when and where the violence will occur.

Cultural diagnosis does not merely *name* a malady or problem (Devereux, 1980). In the radical *separation* of "us" from "them," diagnoser from diagnosed (Devereux, 1980), diagnosis "protects" the larger culture from deeper knowledge, and from the implication of "itself" in what it labels and treats. Cultural diagnosis stigmatizes selected groups of others in order to avoid contamination by (identification with) the stigmata (Goffman, 1963).

From these perspectives, I must conclude that, *at the popular culture level, the widely held doctrine of narrowly bounded individual psychology serves as a defense against recognition of the fact of group psychology and its consequences in violence.* (At the same time, group psychology reflects individual dynamics.) Yet, one is largely ignored, if not censured, if one draws attention to "symbolic" workplace violence, the murder of the human spirit that shaming and intimidation produce. It is as if only guns, knives and bombs signify bona fide violence, that one may not implicate organizational life in goading the person who eventually "goes Postal," as the colloquialism says. Corporate "killers" and "killing" are interesting to the media, and to foundations sponsoring studies of organizational violence, only when the killing is sensational and literal—which is to say, when prevention is too late.

For now, I return to the central issue of this section: What does it mean to have a "cultural understanding" of some phenomenon? There are several—multiple overlapping, competing—meanings this can have. The understanding can be that offered by "natives," "insiders," members of the group. The understanding can be from an observer, an outsider (sometimes even a participant observer who is also a member of the group). The observer, in turn, might try to situate a particular phenomenon (alcohol use, violence, etc.) within the heuristic context of the culture's ethos, its central themes, and even within the evolutionary context of species-specific human biology (La Barre, 1954; Forsyth, 1999).

I do not disparage any local, “native,” or media accounts of the history of the catastrophe “from the native’s point of view” (Geertz, 1983). Nor do I dismiss (by relegating it to “pure” resistance) the work of journalists and of the various news media. Certainly, we stand to learn much from watching and listening, from not imposing an external theoretical map on the unknown territory (Korzybski, 1941). Intra-group understandings can help scholars, clinicians, policy makers to develop better theory and method (e.g., Freud and Oppenhiem, 1911). Rather, I am arguing that any “native’s” viewpoint (including scholarly insiders) *can* serve defensive purposes, and thereby distort the reality it is interpreting.

SHAME, ADOLESCENCE, AND GROUPISH SENTIMENTS IN COLUMBINE HIGH SCHOOL

In this section I explore the role of shame and defenses against it in the Columbine shooting. The emotional setting for the shooting in Littleton, Colorado can help us to understand atrocities on much larger scale. Just as ethnonationalist groups draw upon adolescent psychology and its often-desperate in-groupish exclusivity that guard against regression, adolescent groups likewise draw upon ethnonational ideology to shore up their borders. American urban gangs and school groups may or may not be literally Neo-Nazi, but they often borrow culturally from the slogans, doctrines, dress, rituals, and body demeanor of German National Socialism. Racial/racist theory fits the current ideological need for radical separation, boundary maintenance, distinction of us from them—which in one totalistic (Erikson, 1968) swoop addresses the gamut of preoedipal and Oedipal issues that reawaken in adolescence (Blos, 1962).

For instance, two members of the “Trench Coat Warriors”—Eric Harris and Dylan Klebold—massacred 13 people, then killed themselves, at Columbine High School on April 20, 1999, the anniversary of Hitler’s birthday. They borrowed from Nazi mythology and from Gothic black. They imported Nazi racism and translated it into the American idiom. Themselves “outsiders,” they came to despise ethnic and racial “outsiders” in America. At least part of their radicalism drew from an attempt to reverse and obliterate the shame of ostracism and isolation from their peers. First taunted by the athletes (“jocks”) and the stylish and trendily dressed classmates (“preppies”) as useless aesthetic types who listened to music and liked poetry (“geeks,” “dirtbags,” “faggots”), they withdrew and regrouped into their own counter-cult. An arms race of grudge and insult escalated. Harris and Klebold’s fantasized revenge was long played out on violent video games and on Internet web-sites—and, toward the end, in amassing weapons and building pipe bombs.

Two entries from Eric Harris' Web pages illustrate the link between shame, narcissistic rage, and revenge fantasy (Russakoff, Goldstein, & Achenbach, 1999):

> I will rig up explosives all over a town and detonate each one of them at will after I mow down a whole [expletive] area full of you snotty ass rich [expletive] high strung godlike attitude having worthless pieces of [expletive] whores. (p. A1)
>
> You all better [expletive] hide in your houses because im comin for EVERYONE soon, and I WILL be armed to the [expletive] teeth and I WILL shoot to kill and I WILL [expletive] KILL EVERYTHING" (p. A1)

First called "Trench Coat Mafia" by their opposition, they turned a stigma into a sign of pride. The tormented became the tormentors. The rejected clique became the avenging rejecter. The massacre was a gleeful enactment of the triumph over shame. The two teenage avengers especially despised school athletes and non-white minorities. The extent of the armory—two sawed-off shotguns, a semiautomatic handgun, over thirty pipe bombs, and 900 rounds of fired ammunition—is a measure of the depth of the rage. Harris and Klebold's violence can be seen as simultaneously personal, familial, community, and group-based.

There is yet a further dimension to shaming: the group "attachment" which, in the face of humiliating rejection, is severed, giving rise to intense separation anxiety. Among adolescents, and Columbine High School adolescents in particular, the "in-group" represented by sports-minded and trendy-dressing youth, constituted the yearned-for "omnipotent object" of belonging. Shame at rejection and at being cast out led to the search for another, more powerful, compensatory group object with which to fuse. The "Trenchcoat Warriors" became the local group, which in turn drew strength from Nazi imagery and doctrine. What could be a more omnipotent, and salving, symbiotic "good" object with which to exact vengeance, than Hitler and his Nazi youth corps?

The celebration of *Volkisch* youth mocked the "geeks" and "jocks" who reigned. Devaluation by one group led the "Trenchcoat Warriors" not to repudiate group-isms, but to find a new symbiotic object and forge a new symbiotic tie, one that would reverse shame into fanatical pride. Even so harrowingly personal an emotion (affect) as shame here is inseparable from group psychology: the wish to belong, the wish for acceptance, the wish to separate from the parental crucible and merge with the school group, the wish for protection from exposure—from a gamut of rejections ranging from adolescent cliques to workplace layoffs. Hitler and his Nazi Youth Corps represented indomitable strength amid a sea of weakness.

In his discussion of the developmental tasks of youth, Erik Erikson (1963, pp. 261-262) writes that youth "are now primarily concerned with what they appear to be in the eyes of others as compared with what they feel they are, and with the question of how to connect the roles and skills cultivated earlier with the occupational prototypes of the day" (p. 261). For Erikson, "The sense of ego identity, then, is the accrued confidence that the inner sameness and continuity prepared in the past are matched by the sameness and continuity of one's meaning for others, as evidenced in the tangible promise of a 'career'" (pp. 261-262). He continues, "The danger of this stage is role confusion" (p. 262).

Erikson then continues in an observation that is both contemporary and timeless: He could be talking about Columbine High School, Littleton, Colorado, in the America of 1999. The role confusion that adolescents attempt to resolve in their spasms of totalism is a confusion of identity they also sense in their cultural elders—which is to say, not only in their parents and their past, but in the future for which they are preparing themselves.

> Young people can be remarkably clannish, and cruel in their exclusion of all those who are "different," in skin color or cultural background, in tastes and gifts, and often in such petty aspects of dress and gesture as have been temporarily selected as *the* signs of an in-grouper or out-grouper. It is important to understand (which does not mean condone or participate in) such intolerance as a defense against a sense of identity confusion. For adolescents not only help one another temporarily through much discomfort by forming cliques and by stereotyping themselves, their ideals, and their enemies; they also perversely test each other's capacity to pledge fidelity. The readiness for such testing also explains the appeal which simple and cruel totalitarian doctrines have on the minds of the youth of such countries and classes as have lost or are losing their group identities (feudal, agrarian, tribal, national) and face world-wide industrialization, emancipation, and wider communication. (1963, p. 262)

In this passage, Erikson directs the reader's attention to the perverse symbiosis not only among adolescents themselves, but between adolescents and their parental generation. For adolescents sense keenly that their parental generation is adrift in its own sense of continuity. It is difficult, if not impossible, to safeguard the next generation's identity when one's own is at great jeopardy.

WORK, SPORTS, AND IDENTITY: THE PURSUIT OF PRIDE AND THE DREAD OF SHAME

Further compounding the formation and consolidation of identity is the fact that team sports—high school, college, and professional—share the same core ethos of intense competition and winning that drives corporate business in America. Heady pride at winning contrasts with abject shame at losing. The more vulnerable work-life becomes, the more adults as well as their offspring are likely to turn to competitive sports as symbolic redemption. Berry Tramel writes that in the state of Oklahoma, for instance, "Sport, primarily but not exclusively football, has a major grip on the psyche of Oklahomans. The extreme value placed on athletic victory no matter what the cost has led the state to forsake other worthwhile—maybe even essential—endeavors, such as education" (1993, p. 158-159). High school sports, that since the early twentieth century have been "the great sacred cow of American education" (Zimmerman, 1999), become the battleground for identity, social status, and meaning that the workplace can no longer contain.

If high school sport is, in a way, role "rehearsal" for the relentless competition of the corporate workplace, it is also compensation for workplace failures. Adults project onto their male (and increasingly female) offspring to do the fighting and winning for them that they can only tenuously and temporarily achieve at work. If life does not exactly imitate art, then in many ways work comes to "imitate" competitive sport—where every day is a "new game" facing a "different team."

High school sports—and later, their successors in the "hard ball" world of business—enact and absorb the desperation for victory. Despite the admonition of "good sportsmanship" (that is, of fairness, of placing people above the outcome of the game), Americans "don't remember who came in second place," as one slogan has it. To understand the collective tragedy in Littleton, one must accept that the opposing deadly ideological forces felt equally vulnerable to the exposure and shamefacedness of loss, including loss of status. "Winning," said legendary football coach Vince Lombardi, "isn't everything; it's the only thing." The spectre of losing—and of its associated disgraced status, of being a "loser"—was shared by "geeks," "jocks," and "Trenchcoat Warriors" alike. And it was inflamed from the sidelines by indirect and passive assent.

In American culture and history, ambition to win does not exist alone; it is in constant conjunction with the imminence of suffering great loss (being fired from one's job, having one's job constantly redefined and renegotiated). We speak of "winning big" and "losing big," with little or no middle ground. In this sense, male high school athletes symbolically "run" the school (Zimmerman, 1999) in ways that most males can never hope to "run" the workplace. Put slightly differently, in high school, competitive sports are the medium or language for the deeper cultural metaphor of "winning."

This process places the burden of heroism on the generation of the offspring rather than the parents—and in turn wreaks havoc on Oedipal conflict and resolution. Fathers especially, who can hardly be examples to their sons (and daughters), turn to their sons on the bitter field of sports to wrest narcissistic victory from defeat. Children, who identify with their fathers' (and often mothers') despair, are equally "launched" into the world of high school sports to reverse and redeem it. This intergenerational transmission of the burden of identity defeat is little different from that which fuels ethno-nationalist fervor and terror (Volkan, 1997). It is into this inverted world of responsibility for value that the Harrises, Klebolds, and Trenchcoat Warriors walked—and against which they defined themselves.

TOWARD A CULTURAL LANDSCAPE OF SHAME: REPETITION, PURIFICATION OF IDENTITY, AND REDEMPTION THROUGH VIOLENCE

The very existence of the Trenchcoat Warriors, culminating in the violence of Eric and Dylan's final act, requires the processes of opposition (Spicer, 1971) and inversion in identity, whereby the poles of valuation are radically reversed (Erikson, 1959, 1963, 1968). We can characterize their radicalization as a shift from submission to resistance; from passivity to activity (agency), from inferiority to superiority. The Trenchcoat Warriors inverted conventional values: the drab trench coat, not the latest name-brand fashion, became the aesthetic icon.

Through a radical ideological conversion, those who had been dehumanized now redefined themselves as the very measure of humanity, and those who had previously imposed meaning were regarded as beneath contempt. The non-person restores personhood and dignity to himself (or herself) by depriving the other of these cherished and self-defining, possessions. The denuded becomes the denuder; the accused becomes the accuser; the tormented becomes the tormentor. All these can be construed as expressions of the repetition compulsion (Freud, 1920/1955), wherein one sets out to restage a trauma and master it this time.

Violence becomes a means of that restaging and hoped-for bettering. Hate and violence serve as organizing bulwarks against disorganizing regression and self-destruction. The thrill and joy of hate and violence, such as were expressed by Harris and Klebold, serve as protection against underlying vulnerability and despair. Through violence, dignity is restored by depriving one's victims of their dignity, a dignity first denied them in fantasy or reality by their adversary. Violence liberates the oppressed from the real or imagined oppressor (cf. Glass, 1999). Contaminated with religious and biological ideological overtones, the defiled seek and often achieve purification and redemption through violence. The liberating thrill and joy of hate and violence come to be understood as radical affective—emotional—defenses against total self-doubt, self-contempt, and utter despair. The banishment to nobodiness is replaced by the self-experience of ecstatic allness. If only for a time, "they," not "we," are nothing. Still, the memory and terror of nothingness remains. The arrogantly proud cannot bear their shame, so they split it off, project it into others—and sometimes kill "it" in them.

Time magazine's December 1999 disclosure of Harris and Klebold's five basement-made videotapes paints, I believe, an even vaster landscape of shame and attempts to avenge it. Harris and Klebold had hoped to kill 250 people, not only students and others in the school, but the rescuers and police who would later arrive on the scene. They named the event "Judgment Day," suggesting a metaphysical, not merely mortal view of the slaughter. Had they identified with the wrathful God-the-Father imago? When Klebold said "Peekaboo" to his next victim, was he not (whatever else he was doing) re-enacting the childhood game of hiding-and-discovery: "Peekaboo, I see you?" This is a game in which children repeat and replay with one another the anxiety over being discovered, seen, and exposed by adults? With Klebold, however, the stakes of seeing and of being seen were life and death. The victim would not have her turn at mastery.

I deliberately juxtapose the adult image of Judgment Day with the child-game of "Peekaboo," since I believe that the videotapes offer further evidence for the theory that the planned massacre was, as in a dream-condensation, an effort to right life's shameful wrongs once and for all. Those who had been judged and condemned would now judge, condemn—and execute. Had Harris and Klebold felt already symbolically killed off from their peers' gaze and ridicule? In the planned slaughter, Harris and Klebold would repeat the humiliation, except now mastering all earlier trauma by becoming the humilators.

Had events gone as planned, Harris and Klebold would in fantasy have obliterated as many people as possible who had seen them, and then more. Clearly, they no longer experienced their enemies and intended victims as persons, but as evil things ("part objects"). As an aside, Heinz Kohut's work on "chronic narcissistic rage" (1972) and its concomitant inseparability of subject and object, comes to mind as part of the "solution" to global, total, humiliation. Moreover, Harris and Klebold had come to see themselves as inanimate objects as well. Harris depicted himself as a bullet, a shotgun shell, in a recent English class essay. "Klebold's nickname was VoDKa (his favorite liquor, with the capital DK for his intials). On pipe bombs used in the massacre he wrote "VoDKa Vengeance" (Gibbs & Roche, 1999, p. 44). Harris and Klebold merged (identified) self with destructiveness and with the instrument of destruction (and, as a deadly team, self with other). They became their weapons of destruction and self-destruction.

They would settle *life's* score, not only an individual, or current one. There is some suggestive evidence from the tapes. Gibbs and Roche (1999) write:

> The tapes were meant to be their final word, to all those who had picked on them over the years, and to everyone who would come up with a theory about their inner demons. ...

> Harris recalls how he moved around so much with his military family and always had to start over, "at the bottom of the ladder." People continually made fun of him—"my face, my hair, my shirts." As for Klebold, "If you could see all the anger I've stored over the past four f___ years…" he says. His brother Byron was popular and athletic and constantly "ripped" on him, as did the brother's friends. Except for his parents, Klebold says, his extended family treated him like the runt of the litter. "You made me what I am," he said. "You added to the rage." As far back as the Foothills Day Care center, he hated the "stuck-up" kids he felt hated him. "Being shy didn't help," he admits. "I'm going to kill you all. You've been giving us s___ for years." (p. 44)

The massacre by Harris and Klebold also confronts us with the prospect that such a deed, like war itself, may feel "curative" and "therapeutic" to those who plan and carry it out (Glover, 1933; Fornari, 1966/1975; Volkan, 1988). Murderous rage is a (regressive) cure for shame. It magically annihilates all those whose eyes have "seen" and "exposed" one's vulnerability. As disorganizing as it is to those who are their targets, it is experienced as reorganizing, at least temporarily, for those who are compelled to do it. One can think of this as an *emotionally primitive cure by splitting* and higher level defenses: one defends and preserves the inner sense of goodness by destroying the badness outside. Far from such "acting out" being the "impulsiveness" that the popular imagination believes, it is a desperate, regression-driven, effort to organize oneself and rid oneself of anxiety, even if it means doing so at the cost of annihilating others.

On the broad cultural scale, workplace shootings—now called "workplace violence"—also draw heavily from shame and from defenses to master and to obliterate it (Gilligan, 1997). Transferences operate *within* the workplace as well as from more remote developmental assaults on identity. Projective hatred *of* the workplace occurs synergistically with hatred (psychological violence) *within* the workplace (see Diamond, 1997). Unrelenting social change in the workplace acts like a shortened fuse attached to a supercharged bomb. Defense against the experience of paralyzing shame takes place not only among (1) identified killers, perpetrators, or terrorists, but also among (2) the broader membership of society who protect themselves against implicating their culture in acts ostensibly directed against it. It finds expression in accounts, explanations, and remedies for the assault on society.

CULTURAL COLLUSION AND CULPABILITY

In mass atrocities—ranging from the 1999 Littleton, Colorado, massacre, to the 1995 Oklahoma City bombing, and the "disappearance" of Jews in Nazi Germany—*mystification is the underside of mystery.* The stereotyped response to atrocity is the question: "How could this have happened – and here?" There is a forced naiveté to the question itself. Beneath the veneer of normality, such internal and interpersonal processes as denial, splitting, dissociation, and delegation (unconscious permission-giving) set the stage for enactment. "This" kind of thing was happening long before the fateful event. It is a matter of not noticing, of not acknowledging, of keeping secret, facets of reality. Grief, outrage, and the search for culturally stylized answers are only a part—and a surface part—of the terror.

Public policy plays its indirect role in increasing human vulnerability and sanctioning the very behavior it ostensibly aims to prevent. For instance, in a August 4, 1999, letter to the editor of *The New York Times*, several days after a massacre at two Atlanta brokerage firms, psychiatrist Harold Bursztajn, M.D. (1999), links suicides and violent public "rages" in the U.S. These can be seen as

> two sides of the same helplessness and hopelessness that characterize the responses of vulnerable people to life's fears, losses and challenges. The denial by many managed care companies of mental health care benefits contributes to the failure to treat such life-threatening problems. As we think about the true costs of managed care, we should consider this connection between the lack of mental health benefits and the prevalence of problems like suicide and "rages." (p. A18)

I juxtapose with Bursztajn's observation a parallel one made by family physician Joshua Freeman (1999) in a "Family-L" listserve discussion on the relationship between what is legal, criminal, and ethical in medical practice.

> ...some of the things most harmful to a community and its health (e.g., loss of job from companies moving abroad or being collapsed by mergers, loss of benefits, including health insurance for workers and/or families from companies cutting costs; creation of jobs at below living wage, just to name a few) are not only legal but often encouraged.

Approached as group psychology, the "legal" can be seen as spawning the "illegal," and ostensibly moral (at least moralistic, see Levine, 1999) conduct can be seen as sowing unethical conduct.

A passage by Freud in his essay, "Dostoevsky and Parricide" (1928/1961) helps to situate those who execute violent deeds within the fantasy system of a far wider group – such as "legitimate" governments who condemn the acts of extremist groups, but who quietly sanction them by a policy of non-interference. The large group unconsciously "delegates" its most outrageous, unacceptable motives to smaller sub-groups. Freud wrote: "It is a matter of indifference who actually committed the crime [in *The Brothers Karamazov*]; psychology is only concerned to know who desired it emotionally and who welcomed it when it was done. And for that reason all of the brothers, except the contrasted figure of Alyosha, are equally guilty…" (1928, p. 189).

From what is thus far known about the youths Harris and Klebold, their families in Littleton, Colorado, *appeared* entirely normal—hence their own, as well as their community's, sense of horror that their children, or their neighbor's children, could have done such a horrible thing. It was as if no one knew what was in fact a public secret: that the two boys participated in violent Internet communication, that they were noisily doing "something" in Harris's or Klebold's family garage (breaking glass, sawing, making pipe bombs), that they had guns, that both were irate at their humiliation at school. In such a family and community atmosphere of hysteric naivete, passions and violent actions are enflamed and their expression given permission. In the aftermath of the shootings—as in international terrorist acts—members of the associated groups could dissociate themselves from the perpetrators. Yet, universally, person, family, community, institution, and culture often collude in outrage, only to distance themselves from the identified perpetrator or terrorist.

The struggle *not to know* is part of the conscious and unconscious "management" of guilt, shame, and responsibility. What Fornari (1966/1975) called the "paranoid elaboration of mourning" musters blame and rage in the service of getting rid of anxiety by relocating the source of guilt and shame. The unconscious logic is something like the following: If "I (we) couldn't have done it," then "I (we) do not need to feel guilty or ashamed."

For instance, in Littleton, Colorado, a police report was filed in March 1998 by the Jefferson County Sheriff's Department. In it, among other things, Randy and Judy Brown, parents of Brooks (one of the children killed in the May 1999 shooting), accused Eric Harris of threatening to kill their son. They also reported that Eric Harris had a website on which he described building pipe bombs and openly discussed carrying out mass murder. In a *Denver Rocky Mountain News* article, Kevin Vaughan writes that Dylan Klebold's parents, Susan and Thomas Klebold, "intend to sue Jefferson County for failing to prevent their son from carrying out the Columbine High shootings" (1999). From a psychodynamic view of culture, episodes such as this can be understood as continuous efforts at not-knowing, attempts to displace and project the source of knowing from oneself (and the group with whom one identifies oneself) to another.

A personal vignette is instructive here. In the late 1990's I applied to several foundations for a grant to study the "psychological" violence in the workplace, ranging from everyday *individual* harrassment and goadings (e.g., a supervisor's ostensibly open-door policy that results in punishment of the employee who takes up the offer), to *institutionalized* processes such as downsizing, reengineering, restructuring, and the like. All were turned down for essentially the same reason: that foundations must "draw the line" with criteria somewhere, and that "psychological" or "organizational" violence was not as convincing a form of violence as eruptions of actual behavior such as shootings and bombings. "Cultural," "purely" symbolic violence, was not as persuasively real as the "smoking gun." Here, science and funding follow popular culture. Foundation support can unwittingly, and unconsciously, also "support" not-knowing in the guise of directing attention, via funding, toward knowing.

FROM WAR TO WORKPLACE DOWNSIZING, HUMAN (RE-)ENGINEERING, AND OTHER SYMBOLIC WORKPLACE MASSACRES: CORROBORATIVE CULTURAL DATA

Much speculation in the press and electronic media has been made about a causal connection between the Columbine High School massacre, the technologically spectacular U.S./Iraq Gulf War in 1991, and the 1999 war against Serbia—especially the lure and thrill of mass, impersonal killing, of killing from behind computer terminals hundreds if not thousands of miles away from the target. I wonder how these international events were experienced in the Harris and Klebold families, and their networks, what kind of internal representations they became part of, and what they meant for them personally. (Important as the dialectic of "seeing" and "being seen" is to vulnerability, shame, and revenge in the lives of Harris, Klebold, and their fellow Columbine schoolmates, I cannot help but wonder about the emotional significance for Harris and Klebold of seeing on television a devastating war being waged against those whom one can see on a computer terminal, but who in return cannot see those firing missiles at them or bombing them.)

Certainly, the wars were part of the American ethos, just as are the fear and fascination with guns, the frequent outbreaks of shootings, and the national debate over gun control. The war images were part of the daily and nightly news and entertainment. But I am hesitant to proceed causally from these wars *alone* to the Columbine massacre. The air wars are part of the emotionally-charged, suggestive atmosphere about how problems are to be solved. However, they are not its only powerful examples. The day-to-day world of work and business provides ample close-up experience of these same war-styles, images, and language. If anything, there is even greater *immediacy* to them. The war(s) and the violent computer games have close-to-home analogues in organizational downsizing, restructuring, and other "symbolic" forms of eliminating people (Stein, 1999a). They are part of the same ethos.

I do not wish to *substitute*, say, downsizing and reengineering for war as a way of accounting for the American cultural mood in which the Columbine shootings occurred. Rather, downsizing and reengineering will illustrate how ordinary, how routine, the elimination—if "only" symbolic—of vast numbers of human beings has become within the United States since the 1980's.

As I watched and read accounts of the Columbine massacre, and as I listened to journalists' speculations about the event's precursors, my thoughts kept being drawn to notions of enactment and repetition (Freud, 1914/1958; Hirsch, 1996; Mersky, 1999). Deeds can be "screen actions" (Gadpaille, 1967) that serve the same function as screen memories: to reveal and conceal within a single condensation. There are many ways to kill people. Is there something about the style, the gleeful bravado, the staging or aesthetics, of Harris and Klebold's slayings that can provide clues into understanding more about their meanings?

Let me offer a brief suggestive vignette. Joseph B. White (1996) wrote an essay on Michael Hammer and his popular concept of organizational "reengineering," in *The Wall Street Journal*, November 26, 1996 (front page, right hand, lead article). The article, on Hammer's belated recognition of the importance of "people issues" as well as "engineering issues" in corporate change, gave strong hints at personal issues of Michael Hammer's own that lay behind his organizational doctrines and strategies. In 1993 Michael Hammer and James Champy published the best-selling book, *Reengineering the Corporation: A Manifesto for Business Revolution.* Hammer's celebrated 1990 *Harvard Business Review* article was titled, "Reengineering Work: Don't Automate, Obliterate."

The child of Holocaust survivors, Hammer speaks of "'a common sense of mission'" among them. "'You feel responsible for all those who might have been, but aren't'" (White, 1996, p. A13). Shortly after this quotation, White described Hammer's presentation style,

> Like many a college lecturer, he spices his presentations with one-liners, occasional barnyard expletives and outrageous comments. Talking about what to do with middle managers who undermine re-engineering efforts, he says: "I sort of believe in public hangings for that." Then, assuming the role of corporate sheriff, he points his finger like a pistol and plays out a scene: "What do you think about what we're doing? You don't like it? BANG!" (p. A 13)

Psychoanalytically speaking, it is not "wild analysis" to see in Michael Hammer's role-plays and language a replaying and reliving of Holocaust images. In the present, he has reversed the "roles," and acts not as victim but as victimizer—as often happens with the terrorized who identify with their persecutors, and who then obligate the next generation to "remember" only by first traumatizing them. The impersonal, depersonalized language of massive corporate change, of change-by-obliteration, of public hangings and point blank executions, are from a man clearly with a mission, one in which the unconscious speaks as clearly as the conscious one does.

I do not claim from a single newspaper account to know a great deal about the shaman of re-engineering. I also know that at the unconscious level, ideologies, like dreams, are condensations of many ideas, wishes, and feelings. But, from this single documentary source alone (including its location as a major business newspaper's lead article), I can confidently say that, whatever else re-engineering is, it is also about the symbolism of the passionate destruction of live human beings and not a mere rearrangement of statistics. The ethos and praxis of Hammer's reengineering and of mass layoffs (known euphemistically as reductions in force, downsizing, and rightsizing) are also those of the massacre at Columbine High School.

In a similar vein, as I was writing an early version of this chapter, an ad appeared in the Friday, November 26, 1999, weekend issue of *U.S.A. Today* for the premiere on Sunday, November 28, on cable television station "Showtime" of an original movie titled, "Execution of Justice," "based on the murders of Harvey Milk and the mayor of San Francisco." A large-lettered caption at the top left hand of the ad reads: "WHEN HE COULDN'T BEAT THE SYSTEM, HE BLEW IT AWAY." The ethos of Eric Harris and Dylan Klebold parallels the cinematic fantasy based in turn on reality.

Seth Allcorn (1998), the senior author of a longitudinal study of a hospital downsizing, tells the following story:

> I recall hearing of a meeting in a large teaching hospital that was called to formally announce that downsizing was about to ensue with the help of a notorious downsizing consulting group. The hospital CEO was speaking to all of upper and middle management, approximately 150 people. He explained the downsizing process this way. "You are standing on a train station platform. You have three choices. You can get on the train that is going where I want to go. You can wait just a little bit before deciding what you want to do. Or, you can get on the second train that is leaving the hospital." Since I studied this downsizing in depth as a researcher (Allcorn et al., 1996), I can bear witness to the fact that the metaphorical trains both lead to a man-made hell on earth. (p. xiii)

The CEO is hardly talking in a language of purely rational, denotative decision-making. He is speaking in fearsome allusions, steeped in images of life and death. His scenario is intimidating, inspiring of terror and of historical memory. In recent years I have heard many executives, managers, and workers speak of downsizing (and its cognate terms) in the Holocaust language of selections, queues awaiting terrible fate, and trains destined to death camps. Allcorn's example above is far from rare. It is part of a nation-wide (and increasingly global) psychological terrorizing of managers and workforce into capitulation and dependency on decision-makers.

A second widely used image or metaphor in downsizing is that of the thinly disguised gas chamber. In many workplaces—from hospitals to corporations, from computer manufacturers to energy companies—the modus operandi for announcing a mass layoff consists of the following scenario. At an appointed time, security guards show up unannounced to the office or workstation of the person to be fired. The guard explains only that the employee must come at once with him (or her) to a meeting to be held nearby in a large auditorium or amphitheatre. The purpose of the meeting is not disclosed until the employee is inside. The guard escorts the employee to the door of the auditorium and instructs him or her to be seated. The employee still does not know what the meeting is for. Security guards close the door(s) behind them (some say the doors are then locked).

The room is abuzz in terrible anticipation of some dire announcement. A door to the side of the podium or stage at front opens. The room falls to a hush. The CEO or a similar senior management official of the organization approaches the podium and delivers a brief message: Because of financial emergency, the company will proceed with an immediate RIF (reduction in force)/downsizing/rightsizing. Those who have been summoned to the auditorium are RIFed effective at once. The only way the organization can survive is if their jobs are eliminated. They are not to take it personally. They are to be escorted back to their workplaces, gather their belongings, be escorted by a security guard to their motor vehicle toward the end of the work-day, turn in all work-related keys and cards, and leave. This will be the final day of work for them. The speaker offers some word of regret, turns, then leaves.

As I have written elsewhere (Stein, 1998a;1998b; Allcorn, Baum, Diamond, & Stein, 1996b), this widespread scenario is immediately conducive—equally among those fired, and among those who remain behind—to images of the Nazi selection of Jews, Poles, Gypsies, and other targeted groups, for extermination, and with utter concreteness, the image of being locked in a gas chamber. The style of firing conveys powerful, if unspoken, death wishes. Those who are being fired feel they are being terrorized, not merely dismissed from a job. As with reengineering, if downsizing were a purely rational (as opposed to rationalized) process, it would not be so heavily ritualized. The sadism and brutalization that cannot be openly spoken are overwhelmingly felt. RIFing and reengineering are rituals of degradation and of dehumanization in the guise of reality-based, and thereby necessary, business practices. Bloodless massacres are experienced as massacres nonetheless.

Millions of American workers are the symbolic *desaparacidos*, the disappeared ones, like those of the Argentine "dirty wars" of the 1980's and the Nazi "transports" to death camps. Everyone knows and no one knows. The brutality is superseded by and enshrouded in euphemism and denial (Suarez-Orozco, 1990). Knowing becomes not-knowing, un-knowing. Workers and leaders expect themselves and others to proceed with redoubled effort as if nothing had happened, as if no loss had occurred, to work harder and longer in order to keep their jobs and make the company productive and profitable. People become things rather than persons and turn one another into inanimate, functioning objects.

Now, if these workplace scenarios are played out throughout the United States, and have been so for over a decade, they are likely to have powerful emotional "residues" and resonances. I would speculate that among the most vulnerable types of communities and families are those of socially mobile professionals, members of the upper middle to upper class—such as those who live in Jonesboro, Arkansas, and Littleton, Colorado. Harris's father, a geologist, had entered the oil exploration industry at the time of the boom (1978) and was a casualty of the subsequent "bust." However, my argument-from-culture here is not one of cause-and-effect (for instance, the popular argument that families in which there has been traumatic downsizing and reengineering are most "at risk" for violent enactment). Instead, it is an argument about vulnerability, dread of futurelessness, anxiety over loss, that comes from a shared social predicament and from mutual identification (see Faludi, 1999). These day-to-day realities might not even be spoken about at the dinner table or around the TV set. They are more inferable from a raised voice, a sullen glance, heavy silence, or an unaccountable car accident. Yet they are at least as palpable a presence as the violence in movies, on television, and on popular video games. They are less a matter of directive "child-rearing" than they are emotion-laden communication about hope, dread, and meaning.

For instance, Seth Allcorn (1998) describes the epithets given to some current executives who have presided over massive workplace firings and internal change. They are current, ambivalently held folk heroes and villains, akin to the 19th century Robber Barons: for instance,

> 'Neutron' Jack, a CEO of a larger international corporation who eliminates the people, leaving only the buildings standing, as would be the case if a neutron bomb were used [Jack Welch, General Electric], and 'Chain Saw' Al, a corporate turn-around artist who, as fast as possible, cut out organizational fat [Albert J. Dunlap, Scott Paper, later Sunbeam](Bennis, 1989). These men and other executives like them are the darlings of Wall Street and popular management magazines (Micklethwait and Wooldridge, 1996). (pp. ix-x)

To cite a related example, sociologist Randy Blazak (1999) spent 13 months studying white supremacist "Skinheads" in Orlando, Florida. Despite their range of personality types,

> the one thing they had in common was this fear that the America they had grown up with—or their image of America—was disappearing. And that image was one that was based on straight white male supremacy. Of course, the big issue that also came in was the fact of economic downward mobility. A lot of them had parents who had been laid off from the textile mill or downsized or whatever. If they hadn't directly experienced this, they knew other people who had. They were very cognizant of the fact that the American dream—that everyone will be judged on the merits of

> their hard work and move up the ladder accordingly—was shrinking, a fairy tale. Everybody gets excited about the Dow Jones being above 10,000. But another way of looking at this is how well corporate America is downsizing. It's great for the investors, but for the middle class it's often a nightmare.
>
> The most hard-core kids had experienced some first-or second-hand downward mobility. But the propaganda around the changing face of the American Dream was just as powerful. The perception was that all white people are moving down and all minority people are moving up: "The working-class white man is losing out on America, the country that he built." So it becomes a mythology that is based on reality. (p. 25)

CULTURAL SHAM AND ITS DISCONTENTS

Paralleling the Columbine High School saga, there was, throughout contemporary American culture, a split image between "all is well and couldn't be better" and "there is something terribly wrong happening in America." Usually the former drowned out the latter. In mid-1998, Alan Greenspan, Chairman of the Board of the Federal Reserve, declared the economy to be in the best "health" since World War II. Wall Street soared to above 10,000. Unemployment was very low (I hasten to add that it was deceptively low, since workers were and are more likely to be working at lower wages than at previous jobs, and at work that has fewer benefits.).

Yet in the midst of apparent plenty, there was a mood of scarcity, of desperation, of survivalism. If people "should" have felt confident and secure, they nonetheless felt the opposite. In the midst of this economic prosperity, tens of millions of blue and white-collar workers, laborers and professionals, were imminently disposable, vulnerable to what was euphemistically called "surplusing." Parents of what are labeled "Baby Boomers" and its successor, "Generation X"—the cohort of people condemned to namelessness—alike were (and are still) being symbolically killed off, and were symbolically killing one another off in corporate fratricide and parricide. This process has continued through the economic downturn of 2000 to the present. The specter, if not the direct experience, of precipitous "downward mobility" and of "relative deprivation," assaulted what was left of the idealism of the American Dream (Stein and Hill, 1977), long under siege. The world was simultaneously vastly different from what they, as workers and parents, had *expected* it to be, and from how it was *officially represented.*

In this daily world of work, what sense of self, sense of place, and sense of future, did parents (often both parents work outside the home) bring home? What quiet despair or volatile rages, what disappointment, what impenetrable silences, did their children witness and (unconsciously) identify with—even among the most outwardly entrepreneurially resilient of parents (Faludi, 1999)? This context, I believe, constituted the breeding ground for narcissistic defenses against futurelessness, meaningless, and identity-lessness.

The process of regression, and defenses against psychotic anxiety, led to the consuming violence such as occurred in Columbine High School. In this explanatory scheme, there is no one to "blame" or to "exonerate." My purpose is to explicate the nature of the tragedy.

IDENTIFICATION WITH THE PROJECTILE

Tim Bousquet, for example, offers some suggestive imagery in his "Disorderly Conduct" column in the *Chico Examiner*, Chico, California, May 11, 1999:

> UNCONSCIOUS IRONY can be found in today's New York Times, which reports on further investigations into the Columbine High School shootings. It seems that just a month before the shootings Eric Harris, one of the gunmen, had written an essay for his English class in which he portrayed himself as a shotgun shell. A classmate, Kevin Hofstra, explained that "one assignment was to write about an inanimate object. Most people would choose a bicycle or something. He chooses a shotgun shell and writes about his relationship with the barrel. He often wrote about shotguns." Harris' unnamed teacher was alarmed by the essay, and by another essay written by Dylan Klebold, which described a murder, and so tried to talk with both sets of parents and the school guidance counselor. The Times doesn't say whether the teacher managed to talk with the Klebolds, but said that she did speak with Eric Harris' father Wayne. "Once the teacher learned that Harris was a retired Air Force officer and that his son hoped to enlist in the military, she concluded that the essay was consistent with his future career aspirations," says the Times. Indeed.
>
> MEANWHILE, DANNY SCHECHTER reports on the *Common Dreams* web site that Eric Harris was rejected by a Marine Corps recruiter because he had lied about taking an anti-depressant. Had he been accepted into the Marines, Schechter says, Harris "very well [might now be] on his way to the front lines of Kosovo, the real war he reportedly preferred to fight instead of creating his own. The bombs bursting in air over Serbia and the bombs planted in high school corridors in Colorado may have differed in scale—and impact—but there are eerie parallels between 1999's two biggest news stories." There's little doubt that if Harris' war fantasies had acted themselves out in Kosovo instead of Colorado, he would be called a "hero" by the same society that now damns him as the devil incarnate. (¶ 1, 2)

How do youth sense, how do they make sense of—and what do their families ask them to make sense of—the identity panics of their parents, families, and communities; the expectation if not the reality of loss of life-meanings? What is an adolescent's interior experience of what social science conceptualizes as "relative deprivation" and "downward social mobility"?

When the son of a career Air Force officer portrays himself as the projectile of a launcher, one may legitimately wonder who has set him forth on his mission, what the explosion is about, or the unspoken wish with which he has identified.

One may think of Shakespeare's prolonged adolescent protagonist, Hamlet, who first declares that "the times are out of joint," then decrees himself "born to set things right" (E. Erikson, 1964). What of the father's or mother's Oedipal battles is the son playing out with his dangerous, impersonal image? What offspring depicts himself as a ballistic?—one who had hoped to enlist in the military, and who was not accepted because of a police record? What teacher passes over such symbolism as normal? What adolescent experiences throw youth back on more emotionally "primitive" resources just as they thought they were making their way from family into the larger social world? What scorning, spurning, rejections—projections—induce developmental arrests, identity panics, regressions, and totalistic choices?

In an essay on adolescent Naziskins in late 20th century Germany, Annette Streeck-Fischer (1999) writes on the relationship between the fantasized self and the vicissitudes of the self in early development. "To counteract an impending loss of identity due to an absent, debased or inadequate father, adolescents resort to a more powerful and seemingly more loving father. This interpretation can also assume the figure of Hitler, whose life story of the humiliated and damaged man has achieved a stature of admired greatness and heroism in the eyes of such youths…." (1999, p. 24).

A vast cohort of American youth is currently experiencing the debasing of fathers and mothers in the workplace (not to mention the polemic against fathers and fatherhood emanating from academe), together with an existence of virtual "latch-key" abandonment in families where both parents must work "to make ends meet" and to maintain an increasingly elusive standard of living. In *Stiffed: The Betrayal of the American Man*, journalist Susan Faludi (1999) looks at the consequences for the sense of masculinity of relentless economic restructuring. In social ideology and practice alike, we are producing an American version of what Alexander Mitscherlich (1969) called for Nazi Germany as "Society without the Father."

The son is de facto forced into a maternal fixation, since progressive development into separation from the mother, and into Oedipal resolution, is declared unnecessary! Fathers are disposed of even as they are present. I am given to wonder at group dynamic parallels between American youth attracted to "Trenchcoat Warrior"-style groups and the Nazi youth cohort, as Loewenberg described them in his classic study (1971), sons of fathers killed in World War I or who transmitted to their offspring the obligation to undo the humiliation of defeat.

At this point, a brief theoretical aside may clarify how projective identification does *its* destructive work. A specific refinement of Melanie Klein's concept of projective identification, made by Frederick Kurth, helps us to understand the operation of this process in Littleton. For Kurth (1975) "ontological hate" is part of the self-other relationship in "violent projective identification."

> This ontological hate refers to a negative condition of being set against the sources of life. Put another way, this hate does not allow life to come into being. It positions itself behind life in order to shut off the wellsprings. This hate primordially repudiates any idea of being "behind" someone in the sense of supporting and nourishing and protecting and comforting. On the contrary, to be "behind" someone … means completely to enter into and take over. (p. 325)

In a discussion of Kurth, Maurice Apprey (1993) adds that "Kurth's notion of 'violent projective identification' is … about total annihilation of the other, hence the description 'violent' as opposed to 'massive'" (p. 2).

One may legitimately imagine that Harris and Klebold were targets of "violent projective identification," if not at home then certainly in school (Kurth, 1975). As a target of overwhelming hate, what does one do when that hate is further experienced by virtually everyone around as normal – that the only "abnormal" ones are the targets? Is one not goaded into acting upon that hate, only to be accused of being incarnately "hateful"? In an Eriksonian vein, Streeck-Fischer writes that "Adolescents seek continuity and identity. If they do not find any appropriate perspectives in their family and society, they look for it in the past—in their family's and society's past" (1999, p. 22). In the face of outer and inner fragmentation, ideological and militant extremism became Harris and Klebold's expression of an effort at continuity and identity.

PERPETRATORS, VICTIMS, AND BYSTANDERS IN LITTLETON AND IN AMERICA

The massacre at Columbine High School suggests that perpetrators, victims, and bystanders (Hilberg, 1992) are part of a single, overarching psychologically linked group system that creates and sustains meaning and worth in one constituent group by creating a sense of meaninglessness and worthlessness in another constituent group. In order for sports-enthralled "jocks" and dapper "geeks" to be elevated, someone else had to be devalued. Haughty public pride is a defense against secret shame. In Erikson's terms, the "positive" identity" lives off, and also requires, the "negative" identity (1959, 1968). What we openly repudiate and despise, we also require. If superiority exists only in relation to inferiority, that inferiority must be "made" (via projective identification) to exist, to manifest itself, somewhere. "Jocks" and "Trenchcoat Warriors" are two ideological poles of the same adolescent identity conflict. Winners exist only if there are losers, and no one wants (consciously) to be a loser. There can only be an "in" if there is an "out"—and no one wants to be "out."

Harris and Klebold lived out—and died as martyrs to—the "negative identity," one that was as bound up with the "in" crowd as those who were "in" were bound up with those who were "out." There were, in fact mirror-image identities built upon what Lyman Wynne called "traded dissociation" (1965, pp. 297-300).

At Columbine High School, adolescents played out—that is, repeated, reenacted—the identical win big/lose big chasm that now consumes corporate America, a place where one day's big winners easily become the next day's big losers. The adult big-stakes workplace-"game" of all-or-nothing, built from a Kleinian "schizoid position" (1946) ossified into social structure, becomes projected into high school adolescents and into a theory of adolescence. Instead of questioning the relentless desperation behind the creation of cadres of disposable humans, we instead attempt to protect ourselves against disposability by disposing of *others*. But that only postpones the realization that one could soon be a total loser too—and consumed with its associated shame, guilt, and anxiety. Even wars—such as the aerial war the United States waged against Serbia in 1999 or the 2003 war in Iraq—only temporarily project, displace, contain, and enact this unconscious drama.

I permit myself some speculation. The family is where one first glimpses the meaning of, and the need for, redemption and revenge. Almost as a silent pact, one generation takes upon itself the sacred duty of filling the parental generation's voids—even if it is not specifically bound to loyalty. One may imagine how patterns of identification in the Harris and Klebold households "prepared" Eric and Dylan to aspire to redeem their parents' losses and unfulfilled ambitions, if not their shattered dreams. It does not take "monsters" to produce "monsters." The monstrosity comes from the (intergenerational) obligation to redeem the past in the future. And—to continue my speculation—when the child who bears the torch of redemption is not permitted by his peers to redeem his parents, but is instead ridiculed as an outcast, he is confronted by his parents' (and parents' generation) rage and despair. Perhaps an identity deeper than of success is that of failure (despite initial success). The battle in Columbine High School resulted, after all, not only in defeat, but also humiliating self-defeat after an initial glee-filled triumph. The parallels with Adolf Hitler, one of history's most vindictive outsiders, is uncanny.

By its very nature, "success" in one person or group requires utter "failure," and sense of being failures, in others. Instead of sharing the commonly felt sense of vulnerability and loss, someone, some group, had to come to embody "losers" so that another group could be the "winners." In the massacre, the ostensible winners and bystanders became losers, while ostensible losers and other bystanders became winners—at least momentarily. To put it into a psychodynamic formula: in order for one person, or group, not to *feel* shame (guilt, anxiety), another person, or group, must come to *embody* it – and in turn struggle (alone) with protecting oneself from its annihilating powers. One common form that self-protection takes is infliction of hurt upon another. The issue goes beyond the cultural category of "child abuse." As W.H. Auden wrote in his poem, "September 1, 1939" (Auden, 1965):

> I and the public know
> What all schoolchildren learn,
> Those to whom evil is done
> Do evil in return. (p. 624)

The evil of retaliation becomes the further evil of restoration: if one is to possess a "positive" self, another must be deprived of it. The cultural false self-system breeds further falseness and destructiveness. The need for the tragic action would not have occurred without the complicity of the numerous bystanders who delegate their action to others. What might halt the tragedy is a halting of the need to have someone (person or group) embody and act out the tragedy, that is, a deeply felt sense of "ownership" of the tragedy—the ability to experience inner conflict, and thereby shame—for oneself.

CONCLUSIONS AND QUESTIONS: IDENTITY, ADOLESCENCE, AND SOCIETY

At the beginning of this chapter, I set for myself several tasks to accomplish and questions to address. They ranged from the local to the universal. From this study, what do we know more about adolescence, violence, American culture, and human nature? Adolescent aggression, for instance, at least in this event, is far from simply a quantum of repression, storage, and discharge, but is summoned and mobilized in defense of the vulnerable self and its assaulted worth (see Rochlin, 1973). The expression of aggression in group violence is inflamed by the work of projective identification along with displacement and other defenses.

If I have succeeded in this chapter, it is in explaining *some part* of the Columbine High School massacre. I make no claim to have explained "it all." There is no final, all-inclusive, "all" in psychoanalysis or in social science. Occam's Razor demands simplicity, even elegance, but not simplification. I have not addressed at least two crucial dimensions of the event: (1) the specific, and crucial relationship between Eric Harris and Dylan Klebold; and (2) the interior of the Harris and Klebold families, current and past, and patterns of identification and other defenses that arose from childhoods in these families.

The relationship between Harris and Klebold has strong overtones of many historic and folkloristic pairs where one was the brilliant leader and the other was the loyal follower and zealous "sidekick," whether for good or for ill: e.g., Don Quixote/Sancho Panza, Lone Ranger/Tonto, Cisco Kid/Pancho,

Bonnie and Clyde, and many of the outlaws of the American West. The Harris/Klebold pair seems of the classic folie-à-deux dyad, with dominance/submission (obedience, sadomasochistic) and symbolic homosexual overtones. Much research into their childhoods, later experience, and friendship is needed to understand what wedded and welded them to their murder-suicide pact.

Of all that is written and known (at least culturally known) thus far about the Littleton massacre, there is a virtual void about the actual development of Harris and Klebold within their families. I refer not only to the cultural categories of "sexual" and "physical" abuse, but identity panics, intergenerational transmission or trauma and obligation, real and feared losses, ridicule and marginality in the natal families, and the like. From the five home-made videotapes, we have a glimpse at Klebold's resentment toward his athletic brother, his feeling of being treated by his extended family like the runt of the litter, and Harris's resentment toward the frequent family moves and of the need to start all over again "at the bottom of the ladder." But we need much more to link their childhood and later adolescent society.

Freud has been culturally "domesticated" in the United States, and what we view on our cultural screen about the two youth is mostly screen memory. What we "know" are mostly cultural formulas and fictions, idealizations to defend us against more frightening realizations. We need to know more about the kinds of childhood vulnerabilities that led to the lure and emotional plausibility of specific adolescent-style solutions, ranging from the Trenchcoat Mafia and enthrallment with Hitler, to the actual planning and carrying out of the shooting. We will not achieve these childhood psychohistoric precursors so long as we insist culturally that only monstrous-looking and –acting parents "produce" monstrous children.

The group dynamics of the Trenchcoat Warrior adolescent gang, and of the wider polarization in Columbine High School, drew upon these earlier, and unknown, vulnerabilities, and helped Harris and Klebold to defend themselves against them. Not all Trenchcoat Warriors participated in the shooting. Group process is a necessary, but not sufficient, explanation of the "selection" of Harris and Klebold. Obviously, there is far more critical information to know—and it might never be known. Klebold's maternal family were Jewish philanthropists—how are we to understand his adoption of Nazi lore? As mentioned earlier, Harris's father, a geologist, had entered the oil exploration industry at the time of the boom (1978) and was a casualty of the subsequent "bust." How do these social facts translate into interior meanings and feelings?

Although I leave this chapter on the Columbine High School massacre with many questions, I am confirmed in my Erikson-esque hypothesis about the relationship between "adolescence" and "society." Moralists have long argued that "Society gets the adolescents it deserves." I would argue, by contrast, that *society gets the adolescents it first cultivates—and is then perhaps taken aback by.*

From this second study I turn to the April 19, 1995 Oklahoma City bombing and its unconscious dimensions. I explore it through the symbol and life and death of Timothy McVeigh, who bombed the federal building. The execution of Timothy McVeigh can be seen as a cultural event, one with unconscious significance for McVeigh and for the American people who despised him.

Three

The Execution of Timothy McVeigh

Cultural Mystification and Deeper Clues

In many respects, the execution by lethal injection of Timothy McVeigh at the federal prison in Terre Haute, Indiana, on June 11, 2001, was simultaneously an Oklahoma City, Oklahoma, United States, and world event. His death was the first federal execution in 38 years. It marked the final official act in the cultural drama that publicly began on April 19, 1995, when his truck bomb blew up the federal building in Oklahoma City. It killed 168 people, injured over 600 people, damaged if not destroyed dozens of buildings in a wide radius of downtown Oklahoma City, and shattered the mythic invulnerability of the American "Heartland." In this chapter I shall argue that McVeigh's execution is both a product of American fantasy interacting with his own, and grist for the production of further fantasy and historical action.

This chapter explores what the execution might "mean" and "feel like" at many levels. It contrasts scholarly (and other) efforts to understand, with cultural efforts to mystify—together with the cultural proscription against allowing a villain to be human. It explores the relation between "culture" and "personality," between "group fantasy" and "individual psychology." At best, this study will be incomplete—and perhaps incompletable. Still, one must go on such clues as one can find.

Public officials, media professionals, and interviewees from the American public, quickly arrived at a vocabulary and discourse for the execution. It was "not vengeance, but justice." McVeigh had died "unrepentant," "unremorseful." If McVeigh's deed was itself dastardly enough, its hurt was worsened by his calling the death of the children in the day care center, "collateral damage." His impassive emotion and "defiant glare" during the execution were incomprehensible. There was mostly revulsion at so "monstrous" a being, and relief that "he is no longer on this earth and can't hurt anyone else." There was little public effort to further comprehend his action. As I listened to the televised event and to the news coverage that preceded and followed it, I sensed that McVeigh was no longer regarded as a person being killed, but as a vile "thing" being snuffed out—a very deviant, bizarre, alien *thing*. Nowhere did I hear the word "killed" used. The language was that of clinical and legal "procedure." With his death, there is widespread demand for "closure"—a popular term that was also widely used for an ending to rumination, anxiety, and grief soon after the bombing. The quest for (defensive) finality often makes the ability to learn from experience impossible.

Throughout the trial, the sentencing, the life on death row, and the execution, Timothy McVeigh projected the demeanor of a soldier caught by enemy forces, tried, and condemned to death. From the time of the 1991 Gulf War to the moment of his death, his *personal* identity of soldier-patriot is essential to comprehending his public actions. At the same time, the public and media image of his identity is one of progression (a) from "All American Boy" to "All American Monster," (b) from a "friendly small town boy" (Pendleton, upstate New York) into a "mass murderer," and (c) from a "happy-go-lucky teen-ager" and "model soldier" to a "disillusioned veteran." The "soldier"-persona who bombed the Murrah Building is part of the monstrosity. The two identities, and their discourses, collided (See Stickney's biography, 1996).

Part of the "collision" is an utter separation, within American cultural ideology, between "individual" psychology and "group" psychology—as a result of which any link between McVeigh and the national group is disavowed. This chapter explores both the nature of the unconscious link and of the conscious disavowal.

Recollected facts of Timothy McVeigh's childhood and youth blur into cultural legend, one virtually identical with that of the assailants at the Columbine High School, in April 1999 (see chapter 2, this volume). McVeigh was variously described as nice, happy, shy, talkative, an ordinary kid. Psychological understanding would need to become a stimulus-response enterprise if one were inclined to attempt to extrapolate to the bombing from the facts of Timothy's place in the sibling order (middle, between two sisters), his parents' divorce during his teens, his Roman Catholic upbringing, and the like.

What seems clear from even scant evidence, though, is that McVeigh's search for identity congealed around being a soldier. He enlisted in the army at age 20. In basic training, he met Terry Nichols, with whom he found a mutual love of guns and resentment of any government interference with bearing arms. (One wonders about a *folie à deux* between them.) McVeigh was considered a top gun in the 1991 Gulf War against Iraq, in which he was in a Bradley fighting vehicle. Sgt. McVeigh was awarded the Bronze Star with distinction. He was often observed taking photographs of dead Iraqi soldiers. He was reported to be disillusioned when his application for Special Forces was not accepted. He left the army in late 1991.

During the Gulf War, he was already reading—and recommending—the *Turner Diaries*, a novel depicting revolution against the federal government and bombing of its buildings. Despite his misgivings, McVeigh still continued to fuse the images of fighting for his *country* with fighting for his *government*. In an article titled, "America's Home Grown Terrorist," Associated Press writer Sharon Cohen (2001) writes that in the army "there seemed to be two Tim McVeighs: The disciplined, super-efficient soldier… and the budding survivalist who believed some of doomsday was on the way and rented a storage locker to stockpile supplies." Soon, the army identity and the soldier identity parted ways. McVeigh regularly attended weekend gun shows, at which conspiracy theories abounded. His identity congealed into that of a ("good") patriot at war with his ("evil") government (Levine, 1998). Any previous doubt resolved into psychotic clarity.

With the FBI siege of and assault on the Branch Davidian compound outside Waco, Texas, on April 19, 1993, the soldier-identity completed a radical transformation—one akin to the kind of moral conversion that occurs in religious idioms. What Erik Erikson (1968) called a "totalistic" identity emerged. At least consciously, McVeigh could not comprehend how their own government could endanger women and children in the compound. He gave little thought to the risk that was sown created *within* the compound by the religious leader. To his death, he continued to regard himself as *a patriot, but now one engaged in fighting for his country by waging war upon his government.* Perhaps reality came to match his growing paranoia, one now formulated into a personal ideology. There occurred a radical split between *country* and *government.*

The date of April 19 took on double symbolic significance for McVeigh: it was not only the date of the destruction of the Branch Davidian compound, but it was the anniversary of the beginning of the Battle of Lexington and Concord, which launched the American Revolutionary War in 1775. He had hoped that his assault on the Oklahoma City federal building would spark a second American Revolution. The Waco calamity became for McVeigh what Vamik Volkan (1991, 1997) terms a "chosen trauma," that is, a public event that continues to reverberate with personal, often group, unconscious, symbolic, significance for years if not for centuries. Personal symbol did not serve as, or become, group symbol. There was, to be sure, widespread free-floating rage throughout American society, as can be evidenced by the numerous school and workplace shootings. There was not, however, the kind of *focused* group-fantasy and rage such as had characterized the Cold War.

Public discourse has focused on the Oklahoma City bombing as revenge for the Waco attack. One may speculate that McVeigh unconsciously identified with Waco-as-victim, and government-as-aggressor, even as he consciously identified with the avenging soldier-patriot. Ultimately, as a soldier he not only wished to fight for his country, but—in his own way—to die for his country as well, even if at the hands of his own government. The identities of *soldier-as-victim* and *soldier-as-martyr for his (fantasized) country* help to explain much of McVeigh's later actions, including that at his death. At least part of his inept escape plan can (speculatively) be ascribed to his need to provoke his own victimhood. With so little to go on about the interior of his childhood and of his unconscious in adulthood, one may nonetheless further speculate that the national outrage against him enacted the literal realization of his internal bad objects. His need to punish was inseparable from the need to be punished.

From his apprehension by a state trooper on the interstate near Perry, Oklahoma, on the day of the bombing, to his execution, he submitted utterly to the government he despised. He enlisted the government in his act of self-destruction. One may be forgiven for speculating that beneath the identity of patriot-martyr is that of masochist. Columnist Arthur Spiegelman writes that "McVeigh had described his execution as a state-assisted suicide and he was a willing partner. He was cordial when prison Warden Harley Lappin spent a half-hour with him describing how he would die. He was cooperative when guards strapped him to a gurney and wrapped him so tight that he looked like a mummy" (2001).

For his final statement, McVeigh wrote out and recited the 1875 poem, "Invictus" ("Undefeated") by the *crippled* poet William Ernest Henley. The lines, "I am the master of my fate; I am the captain of my soul," make a call for resolve in the face of great suffering. For McVeigh, final mastery is through death. It is as if in death, he believes that he will still not be defeated, that he will not really die. He appeals, I think, to core American attitudes and values, but now used for idiosyncratic delusional purposes. His choice of poem and poet is a personal testimony. While he consciously identifies with mastery, he (once again) unconsciously identifies with passive victimhood.

His final, "defiant glare" from the gurney may derive from the same source: to see, to stare, while being watched—to die. One must wonder about the place occupied by the struggle between seeing and being seen in his early life, in his unconscious fantasy, and in the dialectic between calmly observing chaos and inducing it in others. The quest to turn passive into active for himself, and active into passive for others, may be a life theme, not only one at the hour of his death.

A personal communication from David Levine (June 25, 2001) may shed further light on McVeigh's seeming contradictions. McVeigh's claim to master his fate

> ...sounds more like McVeigh's wished for than actual self, more like the self he has lost than the one he has. After all, it is an odd quotation for someone who spent so much of his life in total institutions—prison and the military—and someone who is so clearly driven by forces outside of his control, even though they may be forces internalized within his own psyche. It is a very poignant comment, then, if we interpret is as a lament rather than statement of fact.
>
> [This] may relate to one of the most significant aspects of the event, which is the way McVeigh attempts to, and succeeds in, transferring his own feelings of loss, deprivation, and associated rage, onto the families of the victims of the bombing. The great question the whole drama of trial and execution seems to play out it is: Who will bear the burden of loss and rage? First McVeigh, then the victims' families and by extension the larger community, and, after that, who? The loss to which I am referring might well be the

> self alluded to in the quotation. After all, what the victims' families lost, among other things, is any sense of control over their destinies, which got replaced by the sense that they are the playthings of greater powers (the "fates") over which they have no control, and which are not exactly benevolent. Perhaps this suggests something about McVeigh's family. Who knows?

McVeigh's self-ideal could not have been more at odds with his final reality. Hence the lament quality to his resolute protest—an attempt to reverse what was all too real. There is yet another level: if the active *pursuit* of martyrdom in fact characterized much of his later life, then in his execution he may well have *also* been the master of his fate. Such are the complexities of unconscious overdeterminism.

So many questions remain, among them: What early family life and unconscious structure prefigured his adolescent wandering in search of identity, and found it in that of the soldier—and later, the bomber? Of all the catastrophes that occur, "natural" and "social," what underlay the psychological *specificity* in his choice of the Waco assault as core personal symbol? Are there echoes of his childhood in the betrayal and rage he felt at the federal raid on the Waco compound? What is the unconscious meaning of the utter disavowal and revulsion so many Americans have for McVeigh? Is reaction formation, and unconscious identification, in part at work? What can and will Americans learn from the bombing, the trial, and the execution of Timothy McVeigh? How will the survivalists, and the larger American society, use McVeigh's death in the future? What will be the group (cultural) consequences of having destroyed potential new knowledge in the killing of McVeigh?

To great profit, scholars of many disciplines have explored the lives and movements of successful leaders. Psychobiographical and cultural studies have examined the psychological fit between leaders and followers: the dire weakness and vulnerability of the people, the uplifting strength of the leader, and their desperate need for each other. With the life and death of Timothy McVeigh we encounter the phenomenon of what Weston La Barre termed the "failed prophet" (1969, 1972), that is, one whose message and redemptive plan failed to correspond to widely shared wish conveyed in symbolically acceptable guise or form. Far from sparking a new revolution, McVeigh succeeded in marshalling unforgiving retaliation—official and popular—upon a person who wrongly presumed to speak for his national group. Sgt. Timothy McVeigh gave his life for a country that could not recognize him as its devoted soldier.

From this study of Timothy McVeigh and the culture and renounced him, I turn now to a study of the unconscious underpinnings of hypernationalism and xenophobia, especially as they find their way in microcosm into American workplaces. I suspect that the reader will find some uncanny resemblances and reverberations between hypernationalism and this chapter on Timothy McVeigh and his vision of a purified America.

Four

Hypernationalism and Xenophobia in Workplace and Nation-State

INTRODUCTION

In this chapter I explore the cultural work of hypernationalism and its associated xenophobia. Ideological emphasis on creating a pure—and purified—culture constitutes the "crust" or surface phenomenon. Beneath it is a frightened world ruled by psychological maneuvers to rid oneself of all "bad" thoughts, fantasies, and feelings, and to possess, if not merge with, the idealized mother (Koenigsberg, 1975). I start with the more obvious social forms assumed by hypernationalist sentiments, ethnic groups, nations, and religions, and end by exploring the small-scale locale of the American workplace. Taken together, they tell us something vital about what people use groups for.

Every researcher and scholar, it seems, specializes in one sort of unit or another: anatomical organ system, person, factory, hospital, religion, ethnic group, historic era, or nation. The claim of "my world" or "my people" is made by everyone, not only by anthropologists who have spent a few years, if not a career, studying a single group. Intellectual turf, no less than physical turf, though, can get in the way of broader understanding. Fancying that we are enlightening the world from within the confines of a cave, we fail to recognize how shrouded in darkness our understanding in fact is. In his allegory of the cave, Plato, of course, long ago argued this point about the confusion of knowledge and ignorance.

In this chapter I link the studies of ethnicity and nationalism with which I began my career, with later studies of workplace culture and identity. I find that, despite the enormous differences in scale and symbolism, the two have much in common dynamically. Thirty years ago, in the late 1960's and early 1970's, I began my career as a psychoanalytic anthropologist with a deep interest in ethnicity and nationalism. In western Pennsylvania, while studying Slovak American and Rusyn American families and the processes of culture change and retention, I encountered the New Ethnic or White Ethnic movement (Stein & Apprey, 1987; Stein & Hill, 1977). It was a pan-ethnic movement appealing largely to Americans of Latin and Byzantine Rite Catholic ethnicities: Irish, Polish, Slovak, Italian, Greek, Hungarian, among others. It occurred in part in response to the Black Power movement, and its precursor, Black Rage (Grier & Cobbs, 1992). Shortly thereafter erupted the Chicano Power and the Native American Movement, which interwove and alternated between linguistic, cultural, historical, and biological (racial) models.

Far from merely studying the ordinary, day-to-day processes of Slavic American life, I encountered in addition, a nascent, then full-blown hypernationalist movement within the boundaries of the U.S. Among its ideological tenets was a radical distinction between a rabid, destructive American culture and a loving, community-based ethnic culture. The integrationist model of the "Melting Pot" was rejected and replaced by the image of the "stew" and "mosaic"—both of which emphasized clear boundaries between "us" (ethnics) and "them" (mainstream Americans). Love for the inside-group was predicated on hatred for the out-group(s): especially Blacks and a stereotyped, despised group that was given the acronym "WASPS": "White Anglo Saxon Protestants." These WASPS were branded the evil destroyers of all matters ethnic. Stereotyping from mainstream culture gave way to often angry, self-protective and self-justifying stereotyping of United States culture (see Novak, 1971, 1974).

From fieldwork interviews and from ethnic conferences, I learned first-hand how deeply entwined were cognitive and affective (conscious and unconscious emotional) processes, how social movements were infused with displacements and transferences from family onto the national stage, and how ethnonational ideologies attempted to reverse passive experience into active experience (Freud, 1920/1955).

This work on both "behavioral" and "ideological ethnicity" (Stein & Hill, 1977)—that is, ordinary, unself-conscious life and identity vigilance and defense—led to my invitation by the Group for the Advancement of Psychiatry (GAP) for a six-year Ittleson Consultantship to the Committee on International Relations, during which we wrote a book titled *Us and Them: The Psychology of Ethnonationalism* (1987). The committee was first chaired by Francis Barnes, and later by Vamik Volkan, who came to found the Center for the Study of Mind and Human Interaction, in Charlottesville, Virginia.

These all occurred within the American (U.S.A.) psychopolitical context of the Vietnam War, which deeply polarized the nation for over a decade. It was a time during which Vietnamese suspected of being Communist sympathizers were outwardly indistinguishable from those South Vietnamese in behalf of whom Americans were fighting and dying. In the terrifying ambiguity, the Vietnamese were branded as "gooks," as some nefarious, inhuman "other" who could look like a friend and then kill you as enemy. Ideological and political splits within the United States ("hawk" versus "dove") paralleled and fueled those between the United States and the Soviet Union (Stein, 1982a), and that long-lived split within the Soviet Union (and its precursor and successor, Russia) between the "Slavophiles" and the "Westernizers" (Stein, 1976).

The final phase of this period was that of the infamous Watergate break-in, trial, and impeachment of President Richard Nixon—an era in which the boundaries of suspicion increasingly shifted to within the borders of the

United States. The President had his own internal "enemies list." In the hypernationalism and xenophobia of that time, the United States became possessed by a fear of the "gooks" within.

Now, over three decades later, into the new millennium (and *its* worldwide cataclysmic, apocalyptic, chiliastic psychology), the names and localities all differ—but the processes are remarkably constant (see Stein, 1990b). The battles in and for Beirut by rival factions, ethnic and national, are succeeded by the bloody struggle in northern Ireland between Catholic and Protestant contenders, between Russians and separatist Chechnians, between Tutsi and Hutu in Rwanda, between Sinhalese and Tamils in Sri Lanka, between Turks and Kurds, between Muslims, Croats, and Serbs in Bosnia, between Serbs and Albanians in Kosovo, between Indians and Pakistanis in Kashmir, and between Palestinians and Israelis inside and outside Israel. Renewed Jewish nationalist fervor has re-inflamed anti-Jewish coals among Palestinians. We read of "ethnic cleansings" in Bosnia and Kosovo, just as during the Third Reich the Nazis—in a fusion of nationalism and public health in the German organismic fantasy—sought to make the nation and the world *Judenrein*, literally cleansed or purified of Jews (see Streeck-Fischer, 1999; Proctor, 1988).

Yet, all such murderous "cleansing" is not necessarily ethnic or nationalist in ideology. The doctrine in behalf of which the expulsion, eradication, and extermination are done can be virtually anything: religious, political, even organizational. The root from which all group ideologies derive is group psychology itself, specifically group identity panics that lead, via regression, into totalistic images of the social universe and the need to engage in purging the group of all badness. In workplace organizations in the United States (e.g., corporations, industries, hospitals, government offices, universities), under the chronic dread of mass firings (downsizing, RIFing), reengineering, restructuring, deskilling, and outsourcing, managers and workers alike strain to tell ally from foe, and speak of one another as potential "gooks."

GROUPISM AND XENOPHOBIA: US AND THEM

This is precisely why *hyper-groupism of any kind and xenophobia are inevitably linked.* Idealized love for "one's own group" and hatred for the "other" are two facets of the same unconscious process. The mental representations of the other (group) do not exist apart from those of the group with which one identifies self. Unconsciously, the foreign *is* that part of one's self from which one has estranged oneself. In organizational conflicts and in international war, the enemy whom one engages is heavily contaminated with unacceptable parts of oneself.

Perceptions of and action in cultural and historical space enact unconscious conflicts and dramas whose sources lie in developmental time (Stein, 1987). The sense of self is tied to a sense of place that in turn expresses the experience of space: e.g., those places that are comforting and those places that are menacing. Much study of familiarity, foreignness, and their metaphorical configuration in space has been conducted under the rubric of psychogeography (Stein & Niederland, 1989; Stein, 1987; Volkan, 1988).

The end of the Cold War, the collapse of the Soviet Union, and the dismemberment of the Berlin Wall, brought a short-lived euphoria—and worldwide local and regional warfare. The "new world order," which American President George Bush proclaimed at the end of the technologically dazzling Gulf War of 1991, turns out in retrospect to have been a symptom and enactment of the chaos that arose in the rubble of a disappeared bi-polar world. The end of nations, the end of empires, and the triumph of liberal democracy, were prematurely announced (Fukuyama, 1991).

Throughout the Cold War—with its apocalyptic strategy of Mutually Assured Destruction and the prospect of global "nuclear winter"—actual wars often broke out between neighboring client states of the competing Soviet and American empires: Egypt or Syria and Israel, North and South Vietnam, North and South Korea. With the end of the paradoxical psychological stabilization the Cold War had provided, domestic, internal wars have erupted in the centers and peripheries alike of the erstwhile empires. Free-floating anxiety and aggression have continued to search for "suitable targets for externalization" (Volkan, 1988). Only with the September 11, 2001, attacks in New York City and Washington, D.C., did a group—radical Islam—finally condense into the image of a "good enough enemy."

QUESTIONS, ISSUES, CONCEPTS

We now ask anew the questions our intellectual and diplomatic forebears have asked over the past two centuries: which is worse, more devastating, empire-ism or nationalism? And, what are the forces (to borrow from physics) that put this old wine in new bottles? In short: how do we distinguish (culturally, historically) differing and changing social forms and ideologies, from pan-human processes or dynamics? How do we perceive, and conceive of, difference at one level, and sameness or identity at another?

The current bloody strife offers new contexts to address old, still vexing, questions: What does separatism (and separateness, and their dynamically associated opposite, *irredenta*, annexations, mergers) mean, and why do people pursue it? What is the nature and experience of boundaries and borders? How are we to understand what we label as aggression or as terrorism or as violence? What is the relation between events and life in the outer, real world, and those in the inner, largely unconscious, and equally real world of fantasy, wish, defense, self- and object-representation? What is the relation between specific childhood experience, its later structure into personality, the presence of a universal unconscious and species-specific human biology, and the effect of triggering and mobilizing events in adulthood? When Jews and Palestinians, or Armenians and Azerbajanis, or

American Blacks and Whites, refuse transfusion from the adversary's blood, what is the meaning and experience of blood—and of its biological ideology, “race” (see Volkan, 1997)?

One of the central lessons of philosopher Alfred North Whitehead (1925) is the lure and the danger of the “fallacy of misplaced concreteness.” For instance, we look for “ethnic” phenomena in “ethnic” groups, or “national” phenomena in “national” groups. Yet, as the history of society would teach, “religions”—from sects, to large movements, to established groups—often act ideologically and ritually very much like nations. Most obviously, their object of reverence—their Tillichian “ultimate concern”—differs: for religion, it is the supernatural; for the nation, it is the nation itself. Yet, often a blurring and blending occurs. Nations, going to war, borrow magical and moral power from religion (“God with us.”). And religions often lend themselves to national or ethnic ends. Today, in the wake of dissolving Soviet and American empires, religions are revitalizing and forming to fill the voids of meaning and of opposition. Local, domestic wars often take religious form. Religions—and their formative, sectarian precursors—can play out the same “narcissism of minor differences” (Freud, 1930/1961) as do ethnicities and nationalisms. “Minor” difference in ritual attire, behavior, and doctrine can assume major, fateful proportions during periods of identity loss and panic.

No social form or unit is exempt from the processes we customarily associate with nations and ethnic groups: even social class. Especially in Europe for over two centuries since the French Revolution, social class conflict and revolution have enacted all the oppositional group psychology characteristic of nationalism. In modern times, the Soviet Union was founded on a trans-national ideology of communism, one that repudiated both nationalism and religion, yet, which freely borrowed the passionate devotion and ritual from them. The “socialist international” and the Soviet Bloc became the incarnate, reified divinity, the secular object of devotion. It became, in short, a militant, millenarian secular religion.

More broadly, the trade unionist movements of the past century and a half have inspired passionate ties of affiliation toward members and suspicion, if not hatred, toward outsiders. The opposition of “union” and “management” (or owners) repeats in a different social form the struggle between opposing nations or ethnicities. Although dying for (sacrificing oneself for) one's country or one's religion is more widely known, the fact of bloody battles between unions, owners, and the military suggest that self-sacrifice for one's social class, or at least one's union or workplace organization, is quite real.

In the long emotional aftermath of the end of the Cold War, alliances and economic wars between national and multi-national corporations have succeeded and replaced the “simpler” division of the world into the military NATO (Europe) and SEATO (Asia) pacts versus the Warsaw Pact. Blocks of corporate “partners” become economic allies that vie with blocks of corporate competitors. Business meetings often have the excited air of military briefings and strategies for invasion or defense.

The 1990's have long been called the decade of corporate mergers, buyouts, and takeovers, one in which the language and strategy of war, sacrifice, and survival prevails in the supposedly rational world of business. "Hostile takeovers" and mergers wreak havoc with the experience and expression of group boundaries, aggression, identity—all of which are core issues in hypernationalist panics (Sievers, 1995). Just as an outbreak of European nationalisms followed in the wake of French Napoleonic conquests and liberation, likewise eruption of local defensive workplace-based identities occur as the formation of mega-corporations obliterates erstwhile boundaries by mergers and "hostile takeovers." Intense "status anxiety" (De Vos, 1966), with its attendant regressions and narcissistic defenses, accompanies massive social dislocation and the social production of meaninglessness at work.

I would speculate that increasingly larger corporations, national and multinational, are coming to vie with, if not to supplant, nation-states as the "omnipotent object" of dependency fantasy (expectation of goodness), attachment, terror of separation and annihilation, and disillusionment—in short, as social units that serve as massive transference objects. Worldwide process of economic liberalization, privatization, and corporate globalization are making such "virtual" mega-corporations realities as powerful as nations (Rao, 1998). From giant corporations to nations, "the symbiotic lure" (Diamond, 1998) of lockstep loyalty and uncritical thought is matched by the xenophobia of mistrust and exclusion of outsiders.

In this chapter, I wish to focus on the quotidian ordinariness in human society of those phenomena we designate by the terms "hypernationalism" or virulent nationalism, and "xenophobia." Perhaps universally, when peoples look back on their bloody histories, they ask in wonderment: How could this have happened? How could we, or our parents, or our ancestors, have done that or have suffered that indignity? My point is to stress the ordinariness of the historically bizarre, and the bizarreness of the ordinary.

THE ORDINARINESS OF HYPERNATIONALIST XENOPHOBIA: FORM AND PROCESS

To begin with, the processes or dynamics of what we associate with hypernationalism or hyperethnicity is far from limited to social units we label, or which label themselves, nations, nation-states, or ethnic groups. Religions behave in strikingly "ethnic" fashion. So do companies or corporations. Giant industrial or pharmaceutical manufacturers inflate the quality of their products and of their own mission statement—and similarly question those of close competitors. Economics draws upon group narcissism. Within large business firms there occurs similar splits and chronic boundary disputes between such functional units as research and development, manufacture (production), shipping, accounting, marketing, human relations, and the like—each function like an "ethnic group" or "minority" competing with others for justice if not preference, in wage, schedule, and favor.

Small towns on the North American Great Plains act with often exclusivist competitiveness with respect to high school sports (especially football and basketball). Rancor takes the form of pre-game cheerleading, and half-time and after-game brawls. Citizens of many American prairie towns similarly will seek medical treatment in their own town, but not in others—often to the detriment of their health. Likewise, the medical communities of these towns will often refuse to cooperate on mutually beneficial projects.

Intellectual and ideological schools possess, instill, and perpetuate a symbolic brand of hypernationalism and xenophobia. I can cite but a few instances of radical splitting into us/them, good/bad, in ostensibly scientific, academic, circles. Anthropologists have long been divided into "materialist" and "symbolist" camps. Astronomers and cosmologists have deeply personal, implicit theological, divides along the "Big Bang" and the "Steady State" theory adherents. Psychoanalysts and analytic institutes split into mutually exclusive, often xenophobic groupings: Lacanians, Self psychologists, Ego psychologists, Object relations theorists, Classical analysts, and the like. Their derisive jokes about one another is of the same genre as ridiculing ethnic "humor."

The absolutist fallback explanation of "Where I was trained, we thought/did…," applies not only to mental health but to health professionals as well. Often, when a faculty member trained elsewhere joins a medical department (family medicine, internal medicine, surgery) composed largely of trainees from the same university, he or she encounters difference in theory or technique as criticism, and as utter madness: "You do WHAT?" is both derisively said and implied to the clinical foreigner.

Likewise, the ideological specialness we usually associate with ethnic groups and nations ("We are *the people*; you are the barbarians—or at least less human.") is commonplace between biomedical physicians of differing, bordering, overlapping specialties: family medicine, internal medicine, cardiology, gastroenterology, oncology, hematology, and so on. Medical specialties compete with doctrines of their own distinctive humaneness (actual practice is often a separate matter), as if to say: "We are more humane, more patient-oriented, than you." If one must trade with them, one nonetheless mistrusts them.

Perhaps it is needless to say that these adult professional groupisms are heir to the kinds of adolescent identity dynamics that found extreme expression at Columbine High School in 1999 (Blos, 1962; Diamond, 1997; Erikson, 1968; Gilligan, 1997; see chapter 2, this volume).

"NATIONALISM" AND "XENOPHOBIA" AT THE WORKPLACE ORGANIZATIONAL LEVEL

Over the past decade and a half, I have come to focus on the cultural processes within workplace organizations in the United States: e.g., hospitals, clinical departments, corporations, industries, government, educational institutions, and private and public administration (Stein, 1994a, 1998a, 1998b). In both relatively stable times and in the current era of convulsing social change (downsizing, RIFing, reengineering, restructuring, outsourcing, deskilling, managed care, corporate mergers and takeovers), *much of the emotional life of organizations not only "resembles" that of the nations and ethnic groups of which they are an institutional part, but is also, in fact, identical, though in a different form and social unit.* In addition to observing the workplace cultures where I am employed (health sciences center), I have often served as formal and informal organizational consultant. These roles have offered me the opportunity for intensive, comparative, fieldwork.

For several years in the mid-1990's, I was invited by the CEO to serve as longitudinal internal consultant to the downsizing of The University Hospitals in Oklahoma City, a role which gave me first-hand insight into the emotional as well as structural processes involved in a major social form of our time. At the same time, I was involved in co-authoring a study of another hospital downsizing (Allcorn, Baum, Diamond, & Stein, 1996), which allowed me to compare the group psychology at two vastly different sites.

VIGNETTES FROM WORKPLACE ORGANIZATIONS

The following three vignettes or illustrations are taken from fieldwork and consultations I have done in *workplace organizations* in the contemporary United States during the past decade. Some of it is from participant observation, while some derives from formal consultations, internal and external. The material is compiled from field notes, slightly fictionalized to disguise organization and speaker. The vignettes will attest to the presence in corporate workplaces of core psychodynamic and cultural processes found in *ethnonationalist* movements and groups.

Vignette 1: The disappeared workers

In the following vignette, taken from an organizational consultation, Betty, the Chief Financial Officer of a corporation, is speaking to me about a recent "downsizing" (mass layoff) event in her company. Although her narrative and company are unique, they exemplify a modus operandi widely adopted for implementing the quick disposing of employees from a workplace.

> At 9:00 A.M, Friday, security guards showed up all over the plant to the offices and workstations of people who were going to be

> fired. They escorted them to the big auditorium over in the corporate conference center. They didn't even tell them why they had to go, except that it was an important announcement. After they walked them in, they left and locked the doors behind them. The way I heard it second-hand, the CEO then went in after everybody was there, delivered a little speech on how the company had to downsize radically in order to survive and be competitive. He told them not to take it personally, and thanked them for their service to the company.
>
> The security police escorted them back to where they worked, helped them clear out their belongings, then took them down to administration to hand over all their keys and receive their last paycheck. The police walked them to their cars, and that's the last they saw of this place. They weren't to come back. Gone. Just like that. I suppose they couldn't be trusted not to sabotage the computers, or to steal equipment. I don't even want to think about the way it happened. It's like a roundup.
>
> I asked around, and nobody knows where they (the employees fired) went. No forwarding address or telephone number. It's weird, Howard. Like they just disappeared. You wonder if you're next. You try not to think of it. Work harder, maybe they'll keep you. It's ridiculous, because you know it's not true. But you've got to believe that you're valuable to them.

As I have discussed at length elsewhere (Allcorn et al., 1996; Stein, 1998a, 1998b), the style and experience of the firings lends itself chillingly to the widespread association of downsizing, RIFing, and rightsizing with imagery of the Holocaust: selection lines, Doctor Mengele, SS police, and gas chambers. It illustrates the presence of hypernationalist, xenophobic thinking in ordinary workplaces. Brutal action is disguised by the euphemistic language of business. The social "object" or unit of the purge is the corporate workplace. Its survival and "health" (a projection of the biological body, its functions and mortality, upon the group) are to be purchased and assured by the sacrifice of people perceived as disposable. The integrity of workplace borders is as vulnerable and vital as is that of far larger social units. People seen yesterday as valuable and loyal workers, are commonly viewed today, after the RIF, as "fat to be trimmed," "dead meat," and "dead wood"—all threats to the goodness and welfare of the organization.

Whole persons quickly decompose into part-objects. The entire process is at once known and secret. It is executed efficiently to get it over with, once and for all. Badness is made magically to disappear into the outside world in order to revitalize the good objects inside (e.g., to restore the idealized symbol of the maternal-infant psychological symbiosis).

Vignette 2: The Jew in Their Midst

The following vignette illustrates the operation of patently "nationalistic" thinking in ordinary workplace institutions such as businesses. It entails a conflict between a unit director and a social scientist working in his unit in a large Research and Development Institute. The supervisor is a brilliant, ambitious academic medical researcher who is building his own institute and wide regional network. The language of their conflict points to the presence of unconscious issues fueling the strife. In the employee's narrative, the supervisor constantly degrades his worker, often humiliating him in private. Although the employee's ostensible job description was to serve as an applied sociologist on R & D projects, the supervisor forbade him even to use the concepts of "culture" or "society" in his work because "Nobody will understand you." The colleague-employee was widely published in the supervisor's field, but the supervisor often said to him:

> You've published a lot, but very few people in the field can understand what you're saying. ... You keep asking for respect, but you don't deserve any. ... You've received numerous national awards for your work, but they are given by the wrong organizations. Don't you understand that they don't count around here?

Oddly, many of the ideas the employee proposed and championed, and which the supervisor publicly ridiculed or harshly condemned, the supervisor later adopted as his own in projects, grant applications, and publications. When the employee would try to inquire about this mysterious appearance, the supervisor would insist that the ideas were his own, or had come from an entirely different source. He separated, dissociated himself from his colleague's/coworker's influence.

On one occasion, the supervisor temporarily softened and confided in the employee:

> Maybe I envy you a little. I've always wanted to be a field and stream biologist, not a hard driving researcher and administrator responsible for the production of a large group of people. I look at you and I see what I'd like to be: here's a guy who does what he likes and doesn't listen to anyone [an exaggerated characterization]. I sure would like to have the job description where I could devote 50% of my time to writing and publishing.

For a moment, the supervisor allowed himself to identify consciously with his worker. Quickly, admiration returned to envy. The colleague came again to embody what Erik Erikson (1968) spoke of as the "negative identity," that is, the condensed image of all one rejects about oneself and one's internal representations. On a later occasion, while the employee was driving the supervisor to an affiliate R & D site, the supervisor engaged in lecturing the employee as to the nature of his colleague's problem. He was diagnosing his worker's problem, and offering him help:

> What is it with you Jews? You act just like the other Jews I've known. I've never been able to understand why you act as if you're so special. Look at the history of the Weimar Republic before Hitler came into power. Jews were over-represented in government, in the arts, in science, in medicine, in the media, in everything. They were in control of the whole country. Can't you understand why Germans wanted to get rid of them, to get their own country back?
>
> It seems to me like the Jews bring persecutions upon themselves. I know it's terrible to say—and I'll deny that this conversation ever took place if you say anything about it—out the Jews push their way into everything. What happened to them was horrible, but much of it owes to their own doing. It's the same here in America. Jews have infiltrated the government, the news media, the arts, science. They want to control everything.
>
> And you're just like them. You act as if everyone is against you, and it is not true. You get surprised when we push back. I don't know how to get you to realize that I'm on your side. You just need to downplay your writing projects in the home office. You've got to realize that few R & D specialists anywhere can read and understand your papers. Your future here in the corporation depends on your ability to be less rigid and to trust me.

The protection the supervisor proffered was a protection racket. The supervisor had touched something raw; his employee had come to represent something sinister. Hypernationalist (Nazi) stereotypes and xenophobia played a central role in the supervisor's perception and experience of the workplace conflict.

Vignette 3: From Exodus to Liberation—Rectification of Names, American Style

In the following vignette, I am serving as consultant to Union Textile Company, and am speaking with Jack, an upper-level unit manager. He is recounting the recent history of the company, one that entails massive, brutal, social change.

> Howard. There's something terrible going on here in our textile company. Like an infection more an more people are coming down with. Except the infection's supposed to be the cure. It's eating away at us, even though everyone's going around like we're perfectly normal – even better than normal.
>
> About ten months ago, seven middle managers all resigned within a month of each other. They had all worked

together and the rest of us here knew them all. They helped us get through some rough times when a lot of the upper executives were flying all over the place making presentations and showing how great we were doing. Except they rarely were home, and when they came home they had their fingers in everything. That's what's behind the word "micromanage," having to control everything and everybody. It's like they take over your thoughts and invade your body. That's what it feels like. Well, the seven who up and left helped stabilize the place for nearly a decade. They hardly traveled anywhere. They were home-bodies. They helped us to get through a day, a week, a month. They weren't visionaries, just hard workers. They were the grunts who did the detailed stuff. But they got chewed up and spit out. Promises were made—Howard, I don't know the details—and were broken. So were the spirits of these seven.

For months after they left, many of us referred to it as "the exodus." It felt like it. We missed those guys. We felt that they abandoned us. We tried not to think about them, just bury ourselves in work. We were supposed to pretend that nothing happened, that everything was just business. We were supposed to suck it up and make up for their work while we trained their replacements. How do you train someone to become a Rolodex that's worth a billion dollars in contacts? The men and women who took their places aren't bad, they're just not the guys who became our friends. We don't know whether to try to leave or stay here.

It's gotten bad for us. But we're not supposed to feel that. It's supposed to be like everyday's Thanksgiving, when the CEO, the CFO, and the various vice presidents put on white coats and chefs' hats and serve all the employees in line. But it isn't. The other day at a managers' retreat, the CEO – he loves to give Sunday sermons – gave us a pep talk. He said, "You know, I'm tired of hearing people talk about what happened nearly a year ago as though it were a tragedy for the company. We call it The Exodus, The Leaving, The Bailout, The Jumping Ship. It's as though we think we're worse off since they left. That's a bunch of crap. That's a myth. We've *benefitted* from their going. They weren't especially loyal and I don't remember they contributing much to the organization. We're not survivors of some calamity. This is a big opportunity for us."

(Still quoting his CEO, Jack speaks now in a frenzied, triumphant voice, as though a general, leading a charge:) "I'll tell you: Some people call this an Exodus. From this day forth, we're going to call it *The Liberation*! Union Textiles is in for a great future. And everyone here is privileged to be a part of it!"

Howard, I'm ashamed to admit it, but I'm scared by talk like this. The people who left Union Textiles had faults, but they weren't garbage. We're a company, and this is getting to feel like a football rally or preparation for war. It's not the way everybody tries to make it look. It's ugly, Howard, and a lot of us are

> downright depressed. And when we're not depressed, we're downright scared. It's like were a chapter from *Nineteen Eighty-Four. This is America, the United States*, Howard! This kind of thing doesn't happen here.

This vignette vividly illustrates at the corporate (mid-scale group level) many of the psychological processes familiar in nationalist movements. Leadership, with the group's identification based on intimidation, advocates an ideology based on us/them, good/bad, distinctions. A new, radically sunny, revitalizing vision of the group rests upon a radical disparagement of categories of group members, past or present. Shame and guilt are denied and reversed into manic pride, as if to say: "They didn't leave us; we are rid of them." What began nearly a year earlier as a *de facto* purge that drove a cadre of mid-managers to seek employment elsewhere, reappears now as an active, ideological purge to rid the current organization of feelings of badness. They are to be "disappeared" (used as a verb), effaced from the memory of Union Textiles.

Much as with deposed imperial and national leaders, the social valency of these corporate managers is reversed from a position of high regard to one of ignominy. They are symbolically rubbished. The leader, an ambitious CEO, capitalizes on his workers' dependency, anxiety, and wished-for worth in his sight. They identify uncritically with his own corporate plan and with his rewriting of group history. As with shamanic leadership widely (Devereux, 1955; La Barre, 1972), the vulnerability of the group and the destructive narcissism of the shaman are symbiotically made for each other.

An equally radical distinction is made between foreigners (bad people) and the real people (good people). Once familiar people become foreign, estranged, and are re-classified from human into non-human, from loyalists to menaces. Organizational xenophobia serves to shore up organizational hyper-groupism (the workplace equivalent of hypernationalism). "Inside" is purchased at the price or expense of "outside," an expulsion to the outside of those first dehumanized inside. Leaders enlist allies by distinguishing them from clear-cut enemies (Volkan, 1988).

It is, I believe, our reluctance (resistance in the psychoanalytic sense) to classify "merely" symbolic violence with actual violence that leads us to separate ideological Stalinism or Maoism with the "ordinary" psychological terrorism of many workplaces such as described above. Yet functionally, the managerial "house-cleaning" the CEO triumphantly declared is the same as bloody "ethnic cleansings" in the Balkans in the late 1990s.

CONCLUSIONS: RECOGNIZING THE BARBARIANS

At any level of study or social unit—from corporate workplace to nation-state—it is the nature of hypernationalist thought and action to become all-consuming. No amount of xenophobia suffices for protection: for the enemy is unconsciously within. No amount of "cleansing" suffices for renewal. From corporate to national, purges become endless. Full-time attention comes to be devoted to boundary protection and maintenance: relentless xenophobia is one form this vigilance and obsession take. Its self-protective destructiveness ultimately becomes self-destruction—from urban gangs, to corporate executives, to Hitler's final Wagnerian immolation of Germany.

A hypernationalist movement itself is not exempt from all-devouring xenophobia, as the Soviet purges of the mid-1930's, and the final days of the Third Reich attest. The enemy is never entirely outside. Hypernationalism's splitting off of group self-love from hatred of the foreigner is a fragile defense: eventually, even loyalists are suspected of treason and treated as disloyal. Purification can never be complete; impurity surely lurks somewhere. Hypernationalism's destructiveness and self-destructiveness are two sides of the same "coin": the processes of enemy-making that is at hypernationalism's frightened core.

In his celebrated poem, "Expecting the Barbarians," Konstantinos Kabaphes (Cavafy, 1948) describes the dread and excitement within the city gates as the day of the barbarians' arrival approached. As the arrival of the barbarians seems imminent, the entire society mobilizes. When the menace fails to materialize, "unrest and confusion" ensue. The poem concludes with what is at once a lament and a bitter realization: namely, that the barbarians were needed as "a kind of solution."

Universally, much as we despise them, we also need our barbarians (who embody our disavowed barbarity)—unconsciously, we are our barbarians. For group and individual alike, "the other" is essential for one's own emotional stability and internal definition. Hypernationalism and its xenophobias rest upon a degree of failure of differentiation between self- and object-representation. If consciously we hate the enemy, unconsciously the enemy remains a part of the self. As representation, the enemy is an introject, residue of early childhood relationships we have internalized and of which we cannot rid ourselves.

The lesson of any study of hypernationalism and xenophobia for the problem of everyday group relations—from workplace institutions in mass society to nations—is that we can help to reduce "nationalist" fervor and dread in its myriad of guises only as we can come to accept the fact that the barbarian has always lived within our gates—and within that conflicted estate of ourselves. The foreigner we most despise is ourselves in another's guise.

A break in the vicious cycle of repetition that fuels hypernationalism and its xenophobia is mourning (Mitscherlich & Mitscherlich, 1975; Volkan, 1988; Stein, 1998a). In mourning, we finally confront where the barbarians have been along. In place of a group self-image based on absolute goodness and innocence, we recognize and encompass our own barbarity. We less urgently need to collect "chosen glories" and "chosen traumas." We begin to mourn the loss of immortal, narcissistic identity and become born to the metazoan life that is imperfect and will die. Hypernationalism in ethnic group, nation-state, and workplace organization, begins to lose its spell. The darkness begins to lift.

From a study of hypernationalism, I continue in this exploration of "crust" and "core" with a study of disaster, natural and man-made. My point of departure is conventional understandings of disaster. From attentive listening to people's stories, I learn its deeper, elusive, significance. If things are not what they at first seem, they are nevertheless governed by a discernable logic—a largely unconscious one.

Five

The Left Out and the Forgotten
An Approach to Understanding Disasters

> "It isn't what you know, but what you learn after you know it all, that counts."
>
> Oscar C. ("O.C.") Newman, M.D., physician in Shattuck, Oklahoma, early Twentieth Century

> "No man is an island, entire of itself; every man is a piece of the continent, a part of the main; if a clod be washed away by the sea, Europe is the less, as well as if a promontory were, as well as if a manor of they friends or of thine own were; any man's death diminishes me, because I am involved in mankind; and therefore never send to know for whom the bell tolls; it tolls for Thee."
>
> John Donne, *Devotions*, 1624 (Bartlett, 1955, p. 218)

INTRODUCTION

The occasion for this chapter was the first conference held by the Worcester (Massachusetts) Institute on Loss and Trauma, held October 20, 2000. December 3, 2000, would be the first anniversary of a fire that consumed the Worcester Cold Storage and Warehouse Company and took the lives of six firefighters. The fire was started by two homeless people who had been living in the building. Accidentally, they knocked over a candle, could not put out the fire themselves, and left the building without reporting the fire. This chapter is about that disaster, and about understanding and responding to any disaster—however it comes to be defined and experienced, however short or long it lasts.

The October 20, 2002, conference was devoted to understanding the December 3, 1999, fire; thus, whatever else it was, it was part of the disaster and the response to it. Moreover, the conference speakers and attendees were writing and rewriting the story of the disaster, asking: How long does a fire burn, symbolically speaking? How do we deal with a fire we have already been burned by—some literally, some symbolically? How do we deal with the twin temptations of "becoming" the fire, ourselves, and insisting that we were not even "singed" by its far-reaching flames?

This chapter addresses these simultaneously urgent and timeless questions about the Worcester fire and about any disaster. Reality is lumpy cream of wheat, always aesthetically imperfect. We often omit this lumpy reality from our scholarly accounts and clinical strategies. As a consequence, practically speaking, real people (individuals, groups, categories of people) get left behind because we fail to notice them or to grant them a place in our drama. They are, in effect, abandoned to their own grief and resourcefulness. This is part of the price we all pay for overly homogenized, stylized cream of wheat. This chapter explores the experiential world beneath culturally encrusted accounts of disaster. It attends to the many levels of disaster narratives. What is in the core turns out to be vastly different from what is on the surface. The surface omits and forgets many crucial elements in a disaster. As in early chapters, this one is also about recent American culture and memory.

OPENING STORIES

I begin with two brief stories about disaster. I teach an annual seminar called "behavioral sciences in occupational medicine" to physicians and physician associates (P.A.s). Over its seventeen weeks I invite several speakers to teach us about the real world. One of these is a P.A. who is the occupational health manager for the City of Oklahoma City. Prior to P.A. school, he was a firefighter, from which he retired after many years of service. The date of class was March 3, 1997. Early in his talk he described a fire in which three Oklahoma City firefighters had died in 1989. His account went something like this: "There was a flashover and backdraft. These were the first deaths in the Oklahoma City Fire Department since the 1950's. 1989. *TODAY*! March 3, 1989." Having started to *tell* a remembered story, he suddenly found himself *re-living* it. His pupils were, for the moment, dilated and fixed in the distance, nowhere in the classroom. For a few seconds there was utter silence in the room. He then re-composed himself and continued with his part in the three-hour seminar.

Suddenly, a portion of a talk about memory and disaster becomes a moment in traumatic remembering itself. He was far enough away in time from the original event not to be conscious of the anniversary date. Yet, in the unconscious, the event was still emotionally volatile, and as soon as he recognized the date, he was briefly swept up in the narrative rather than simply recounting it.

A second story:

The following story is parable and metaphor for what I have learned about understanding disasters and helping people afterwards. Much of what is most important, short term and long term, is not immediately obvious from direct vision. It rather comes more via peripheral vision—from the corner of the eye. It takes us unprepared precisely as the calamity itself once did. I do not dispense with our official clinical and crisis intervention categories and methods, but I question their ability to contain "the whole story," especially one that continues to emerge. Philosopher Alfred North Whitehead long ago stressed, "Seek simplicity and mistrust it." In life as in medicine and science, there must be a healthy tension between rules and exceptions.

Around two and a half years after the bombing of the federal building in Oklahoma City, a University of Oklahoma Health Sciences Center faculty physician colleague was taking family medicine residents on a community medicine rotation at a local clinic for indigent patients. In a getting-acquainted fashion, the faculty physician was talking with the clinic nurse about her work and experience. At one point, she asked her whether she had been involved in the medical community's response immediately after the bombing. The nurse burst into tears, and a geyser of feelings and memories erupted. My colleague said that the nurse talked and talked, as if for the first time. She said that 2 ½ years ago, no one had "debriefed" her and asked what *she* had gone through. After volunteering some time to the emergency effort, she returned to her work, which everyone treated as "business as usual." Because she had not been in or around the buildings immediately after the bombing, she did not occupy the mental and linguistic category of "victim" or "survivor" or "hero." Certain kinds of people were regarded as having been as "traumatized." Others simply pitched in to help.

The occasion that unleashed memory and emotion was my colleague's simple expression of interest in her possible role in the bombing-recovery effort. My colleague, Allene Jackson, M.D., had been one of the early responders to the bombing site and had learned to inquire in this manner. The occasion was not an "anniversary"-style reaction, but, like the first story above, a crucial ingredient was similar: an event in the present strongly resembled a catastrophic event in the past and provided the environmental "stimulus" for the release of unconscious memory and affect. To quote Whitehead again, "Seek simplicity and mistrust it." Especially when dealing with catastrophes, it is difficult not to seek simplicity and to take comfort in it, for it feels as if the world is falling or ripping apart.

THINGS ARE NOT WHAT THEY SEEM

Substantively, this chapter studies disaster, the human experience of disaster, the social construction of disaster, and the contribution of applied anthropology to being useful following disasters. *Methodologically*, this chapter explores anthropologically generic (a) *epistemological* issues (What we know is founded on how we come to know.); (b) *ontological* issues (fidelity to data and to learning from experience versus fidelity to theory and method); and (c) *relational* issues (learning from and with others in the very process of "applying" what we know). This chapter adds further dimensions to ongoing insider and outsider understandings of culture(s) and culture change, and to the necessary tension between intensive case study and comparative study. Finally, this chapter can be situated at the intersection between theory, praxis, and ethics.

In disasters or catastrophes as in the rest of life and culture, *things are not what they seem*. They are not what we want and need them to be. Further, *despite our claims to learn from experience, we often do not* (Bion, 1962). More often than not, we impose our narrative and ideological order on experience. In disasters, as in life, we often think we know, and act, before we ask. We often get in the way and label it "being helpful." Our fidelity is often more to a theory and method than to the phenomena themselves.

We say, for instance, that we wish to be of help—in better understanding disaster, in helping those overwhelmed by it. Do we assume entirely that we know how to be of help and that we merely need to ply our trade? Or do we also *learn from those whom we are helping* as we are offering our assistance?

Part of the getting-in-the-way is the American cult of the expert, the One Who Knows, the one who presumably possesses god-like "expertise." Whatever in fact any "expert" really knows, the expert in fact is a person who is projectively imbued with and embodies the wished-for omnipotence and omniscience in the vulnerable group—which is what charismatic leadership is all about (Devereux, 1955; La Barre, 1972). By contrast, I suggest that authentic ability is not necessarily an inherent or projected property of a person, magically endowed. It is rather the intersubjective dance of relationship in which all participants bring out the best in each other and step beyond a victim/victimizer mode. Ultimately, I do not have "the answer" or all of "the answers." I bring what I know, but so does the reader. I help to foster an environment of emotional safety in which new answers have the possibility of emerging—from many people who are working together. We Americans tend to solve urgent problems by attacking and descending on them—and the people who have them—with armies of experts. There is a more respectful, inclusive, way of "getting the job done."

From firefighter and policeman to doctor and social worker, perhaps the ancient notion of the "wounded healer" is closer to who and what helps in the long run rather than the persona of invulnerability inherent in the man or woman "made of steel." Knowing our woundedness, and access to it, is part of our strength, though from the point of view of our defenses, we and clients often insist that it is only a sign of (moral) weakness.

One might reply that in emergency situations, one must be prepared to respond immediately, that there is not the luxury of reflective thought. I do not quarrel with emergency response as a general idea – so long as we are attuned to reality. I do have questions when part of the emergency is our own erupting anxiety that we try to quell through "doing something," usually dramatic, immediately. In this chapter, this will be my central theme amid many variations. It is important to know when the main problem we are trying to solve is our own anxiety. And that anxiety often clouds our understanding of very basic things. The effort to be "made of steel" often compromises our ability to think, to feel, and to respond.

We Americans have clinical and cultural notions of "crisis management" and "incident management" the same way that we have notions of *managing*—that is, controlling—virtually anything. Through language and ritual, we often engage in magical thinking and acting. Some trauma, disaster, or catastrophe is utterly unimaginable (e.g., the 1995 Oklahoma City bombing); other is thinkable (e.g., a tornado, hurricane, or flood), but usually not with respect to *us*. In either case, we are at least in some respects utterly *unprepared* for what befalls us. Yet, when we are overwhelmed by something, we wish not only to be better prepared in the future, but to magically reverse the past as well. That is, the wish is to re-master the past in the future. Part of what is so frightening about disaster—which is to say the subjective, as contrasted with the objective, side of it—is that it first takes us by surprise and then seems to "possess" us. It is hard to fight demons when they are also inside us.

Each disaster occurs within the "fabric" of how we view the world and how we expect the world to "go." In 1950, Immanuel Velikovsky created quite a stir among cosmologists, geologists, astronomers and other intellectuals in his assertion that the history of the earth and of the solar system has been one ridden by cataclysm, and not one ruled by uniform, incremental change. Dramatic change, not perfect Laplacian function, is the rule. However one judges the cosmological theories and evidence of Velikovsky (1950), he points at a central official tenet of western civilization: that things go mostly smoothly, that things belong and stay in their place, that change is slow, gradual, and incremental. Only in the past few decades have social scientists begun to recognize that even *massive cultural change might be ordinary rather than historically exceptional.*

The implication of this debate for disaster and adaptations to disaster, is that while *objectively, disasters are not infrequent, subjectively, disasters feel infrequent.* More precisely, disasters rarely befall us, but only if the "us" is defined and bounded narrowly. Part of the issue is the unit of affiliation, that is, those who feel that the disaster is or was theirs. Who owns it? Whose fire, flood, or bombing is it? How narrow or broad is identification with, or influence by, the disaster? The intensive *case study method* and the *comparative method* complement each other and help us to sort out what is local, what is universal, and how we might learn from each other how to be of help (see Ablon, 1973; Erikson, 1976; Kleinman, Das, & Lock, 1997; Kluckhohn & Strodtbeck, 1961; Krystal, 1988; La Barre, 1972; Luel & Marcus, 1984; Oliver-Smith, 1992; Stein, 1995, 1999b; Terry, 1984; Volkan, 1988; Young, 1996).

I do not say this in order to smuggle in fields such as anthropology, sociology, political psychology, or psychohistory as having *the answer*, for we would be back in the same place I first identified as a *cul de sac*. I less advocate a specific field or assortment of fields, than I suggest that a theory or method is valid and ethical insofar as it honors the experience of people as a place of departure and of reference. It is not the only view, but it is an essential one. It is also one that the history of science, even social science, most dreads (Devereux, 1967). The code words that describe the approach I advocate include: story, narrative, listening deeply, attending to others, phenomenology, careful observation, intersubjectivity, experience (see Brody, 1987; Gabriel, 2000; Kleinman, 1988; Mattingly 1998; Stein & Apprey, 1990). Most of all, fidelity to what makes us most uncomfortable.

EVENT, LANGUAGE, AND STORY

A disaster is an *event*, and a disaster is a *language*. In their outward contours, some disasters are brief, acute, while others are long-lived, chronic. Over time, a disaster can become a language that hijacks an event. A disaster is a story, a set of stories, an evolving story, about an event, *after* an event. A disaster is also a kind or type of story line about an event, one that *precedes* an event. The story line is replete with characters, plot, sequence, structure, and the "right" kind of ending. A story line or "narrative" is a form we use to say how a story—and its event—*should* go. There are story lines for how a "good fire" or a "good bombing" goes, and for how heroes, healers, and the public respond.

In a disaster and its accounts, there are categories of people, categories of time, categories or types of timetables. Certain categories of people are publicly recognized, acknowledged; certain other categories of people are publicly unacknowledged, overlooked, ignored. Some categories of people court publicity, while others shy away from it. Some are discountable, whether in heroism, suffering, or even memory (Javors, 2000; Doka, 1989). Who counts? Who is treated as though they do not matter? Who is remembered? Who is forgotten? Who is, or becomes, a social symbol, even a "social cynosure" (La Barre, 1946), a category of persons to whom much attention is devoted? What are the costs to each? When the armies of Montgomery and Rommel fought in North Africa during World War II, who gave much thought to the Bedouins who were caught in the clash of worlds? In disasters, who gets left out, and what becomes of them?

There are public stories of heroism. There are private, secret, stories, often at odds with those that are told and retold. There are many kinds of suffering: speakable, unspoken, unspeakeable. Many people get left behind.

Many stories are only partially told, if even partially. Many stories are undiscussable. Can "heroes" have flaws, or must they have perfection? Can heroes have extramarital affairs or drink alcohol to excess, or abuse their spouses and children, or cheat on income tax returns? Can heroes be among the living, or must they be sacrificially dead? What do we do with what *is*, but which *cannot be*, because it is so intolerable, unthinkable? When we—as professionals, as lay people, as ordinary citizens—read and write stories of catastrophes, we are often more faithful to the way "things *should* go" (which is always someone's view) and to our methodologies than to the phenomena we are trying to understand and the people we are trying to help (Ritzer, 2000). We even have expectations about how disasters themselves *should go*: e.g., what a good fire and what a bad fire are. Part of the terror is when "the perfect fire" goes bad (Flynn, 2000).

To use my earlier metaphor: If we are more faithful to *smooth* cream of wheat than to the more ordinary and distasteful *lumpy* variety, what happens when the world serves itself up to us lumpy? Can we accept the "lumpiness" as part of the given—to understand, within which we try to help—or do we insist that what is before us is smooth? The image would seem to pervade many facets of our response to disaster.

Individuals, organizations (fire and police departments, hospitals, clinics), and whole communities often take pride in their response to a catastrophe. Community pride can rest on a simple, fundamental sense of goodness of place. It can also rest on feelings of inadequacy and shame that can never be expunged, a badness that cannot be erased. There often lingers a secret shame and guilt that the calamity happened at all, that it happened in this place, that we should have done differently or better.

Some people have asked, directly or indirectly: How dare the 1995 bombing take place in the "Bible Belt"—and by someone who is not identifiably "foreign"? In Worcester, where many citizens aspire to a higher status and self-image for their city ("Paris of the 1980's" vs. "ageing mill town" and "New England's utility closet"): how might the 1999 Worcester fire feel like an affront to the community as well as, in the response to it, a source of pride to be a New Englander? A disaster, and the response to it, may feel, for a while redeeming, as if it suddenly put a place "back on the map" as a good place rather than as a backward or deficient place. The disaster can become a part of redefining a person and community's sense of place (see Feld and Basso, 1996; Fullilove, 1996). Conversely, *where* something happens is part of the "happening," the eventfulness itself. To repeat a theme of this chapter: things are not what they seem.

There is an abundance of studies of "cultural bereavement" (e.g., Eisenbruch, 1984a, 1984b, 1991, 1992; Stein, 1978) with respect to such large social categories as ethnic groups, nationalities, and religious denominations. But far less attention has been paid to such more local place units as, say, states/provinces, cities, towns, communities, workplaces, work groups, military battalions, and the like. Yet the sense of loss occurs everywhere people develop and define a sense of "we-ness," from a fire station to a factory or union. Some losses are publicly recognized, and others are not. In the process, those of us in the "helping" professions miss and overlook a great deal of grief because grief does not happen to the "right" categories of people. There are many styles, rites, and narratives of loss and grief that we have not bothered to learn.

The challenge, I believe, is to *listen to the people whom we are trying to help*, better than we listen to our theories and methods. We need to ask, to wonder, "What is it like to be you?" What I happen to think a trauma looks like, how long I think it should take to "heal" or to "get over it and get a life," how I think resolution occurs, may differ from how you see or how you think about time. Now, as an anthropologist I don't think that the "native" is always right; nor is the helper or consultant. But one starts somewhere, and respectfulness begins with listening, observing, attending.

Consider two terms widely used in association with mass disaster: "survivor syndrome" and "debriefing." The former term was developed by psychiatrist and psychoanalyst William G. Niederland from his work with survivors of the World War II Holocaust (1961, 1964). It refers to the often unconscious sense of guilt, and chronic anxiety, experienced by many people who lived while so many of their family had perished in the death camps. Through its usage in increasingly wider clinical and popular circles, *interpretation based on inference from data insidiously "becomes" the data themselves.* All "survivors" become presumed to possess and to evidence the "syndrome" that characterizes them (cf. Terry, 1984). Ironically, a felicitous concept that began with serious listening turns into a cultural sign of a failure to listen and a prescription for that failure. One purports to "know" people even before one hears them. Explanation becomes sacrificed for projection. It becomes difficult if not impossible to know who suffers from the survivor syndrome if we assume that everyone does, and equally so.

The second term, "debriefing," is widely employed by practitioners of Critical Incident Stress Debriefing/Management. It derives from the twin military terms of the official "briefing" of combatants prior to battle or another military "operation," and of "debriefing" them afterwards. In relation to disaster, victims and disaster workers are expected to "debrief" DISD/M practitioners about their highly emotional experiences immediately after their involvement a catastrophe in order to prevent subsequent post-traumatic stress disorder (PTSD). Medical colleagues involved in responding to the Oklahoma City bombing, to tornadoes, and to day-to-day clinical encounters, often approach me and say, "I need to debrief to/with you." I am expected (reciprocally) to understand the request, to stop what I am doing, and to listen. Even though I question much of the theory and methodology of CISD/M, I accept my colleagues' need to talk, to be heard, and I accept their choice of me as a person whom they trust. Because they can label whatever intersubjectively takes place between us as "debriefing," they can, among other things, save face in not having to label it something beyond emergency management. In short, I accept their cultural term and offer my help within it.

ANNIVERSARY REACTION AND "PERCEPTUAL IDENTITY"

The widespread clinical concept of the "anniversary reaction" or "anniversary syndrome" can also be situated more broadly in culture and language than strictly within the realm of health and mental health. I concur with "clinical wisdom" that it is certainly important for individuals, families, clinicians, organizations, and communities to be alerted for physical, emotional, and behavioral volatility as an anniversary date of a catastrophe approaches and occurs. The concept may help to explain the timing and intensity of the reaction. But if we think only in terms of the cultural category, "anniversary reaction," we see the trees but miss the forest, as it were. When "anniversary reaction" becomes obligatory folklore, it loses explanatory power as science. We think very concretely about the anniversary date and forget the more general issue of a contemporary "trigger" or environmental precipitant evoking a return of what is repressed or split off. It is less the anniversary per se as it is *the anniversary as an exemplar* of something or of events in the environment that releases the repression or splitting, and that becomes the occasion for regression.

The core issue is not "time" alone, but resemblance between present and past. Freud's (1900/1953, pp. 566-567) notion of the "perceptual identity" between the current event and the one earlier repressed helps us to understand that there may be a vast array of environmental cues, in space and in time, that may act as "triggers." This realization does not diminish the importance of thinking about "anniversary reactions." Rather it situates these reactions within a far broader range of times and places and persons that might lead to the same physical, emotional, or behavioral eruption.

For a brief example, several clinician colleagues told me one morning during March 2000 how they had been spooked the previous night by the very dark hue of the sky and by the severe weather warnings. Why *haunted*? "Because it looked like the tornadoes of May 3, 1999, that ripped through central Oklahoma." Our clinical and therapeutic inquiries should include anniversaries, but we should broaden them to include resemblance, as in the question: "Is there anything in what you're experiencing now that was at all *like* something terrible you went through in the past?"

LEARNING TO HELP AS WE TRY TO HELP

In short, *can we learn from the very people we are trying to help, even as we are helping them?* Can we let them help us to help them? Put differently, how can we help people feel understood, whose inner and outer worlds have become disorganized? Could we, the responders or caregivers, overly *organize* ourselves with methods and techniques *in order to* avert feeling disorganizing anxiety in ourselves?

In the days following the federal building bombing in Oklahoma City, workers in some of the buildings immediately affected by the explosion were gathered in mandatory "debriefing" sessions ranging from one to several hours in length. They were encouraged to express their feelings in the group and told that the wide range of feelings they would have in the near future were normal. Several people who had been in the federal building and in the Journal Record building across the street (as well as in other nearby buildings) told me that they thought these debriefings were a waste of time, at least at the time. What would have been far more helpful to them, they continued, was for people not to take them away from work but to help them put their world together again. They needed help in moving to new, strange work sites. They wanted to get their computers and other equipment going again. In short, as I have discussed elsewhere (Stein, 1999b), the Oklahoma and wider prairie work ethic served the purpose of mastery in the face of cataclysm. At least for the moment, getting back to work felt like healing, not like the avoidance of healing.

One person—who would have been killed had he been in his actual office at the time of the explosion—kept finding slivers of glass in his filing cabinets and in his books. He carefully took each one and collected them all in a small compartment in his top desk drawer. On the one hand, he was eager to return to work and try to put his world together again, via working. On the other hand, he was symbolically memorializing the bombing by putting and keeping all the reminders of the explosion in one familiar place.

It is not easy. In time of great pressure to "Do something," to intervene, when we want answers to questions driven by intense anxiety about death or aggression or sexuality or vulnerability, *can we tolerate to learn as we go*, to learn even as we are "doing"? Can I afford to make you more important than what I think I already know best? Can I learn partly from you what I should do to be helpful? Can I listen at least as well as I talk? Can what I say come from first having listened to you before I decide what to say and how to proceed?

Both with respect to the 1995 Oklahoma City bombing and in the 1999 Worcester fire, I have heard people say, either directly or in effect: "We, who *don't have* these kinds of problems, *have* these kinds of problems. What becomes of us now?" People respond not only to events as singular events but to events as symbols. When an event comes to represent something, often two interrelated disasters must be faced: the event itself, and what it means. How, people ask, can something happen here that doesn't happen here? The fact *that it happened* may be as crucial a part of the trauma as *what* specifically happened. This approach to disaster is more carefully nuanced than one that explains experience and memory exclusively as properties of the event (McNally, 2003; Stein, 1996b, 1997a, 1997b).

Many questions come to mind that can help us to understand how people experienced what happened to them: What kinds of things do people do to help themselves and each other? What do they say as their needs? Can we start here rather than only with our own truths and solutions? Can we not just label others' response, as say, "denial" or some other technical or psychiatric term, but instead start where they are, with how they *experience* the disaster, rather than with where we want them to be?

In psychoanalysis at its ideal and best, the therapist approaches each session with an attitude of what Freud called "evenly suspended attention" *("gleichschwebenden Aufmerksamkeit")*(1912/1958, pp. 111-112) (as in the image of a fulcrum balancing two plates on a scale). The attitude of attentive not-knowing best characterizes the consultant and applied social scientist who is trying to be of help after disaster. Such an approach helps to correct the tendency to "apply" our favorite theories. Consider an example from a highly popular "cognitive" approach to mental functioning. Shelley Taylor (1983) proposes a theory of "cognitive adaptation," whereby people come to terms to threatening events via certain strategies. This adaptation involves the search for meaning, the attempt to gain control, and the effort to rebuild one's self-image.

What, however, is the process of adaptation if it extends beyond individuals to families, communities, whole cultures? Is the entire process a strictly "cognitive" one? What of the feelings of loss, of rage, of despair, and of the numerous forms mourning takes? Are these, too, not part of adaptation? Does not emotion color all perception and cognition? What, in this model, is the place for futility and fatalism, as well as active mastery? What do we make of a wide, if not universal, tendency to attempt to turn a passive, victimizing experience into an active one, in fact restaging the menace in a new, later, disguised form? Where does repetition fit into this rational scheme—and where does reason fit into the process of repetition? What vulnerabilities did the self-image (person, group, place) have prior to the current threat to it? If theory other than a strictly cognitive one raises some of these issues, the sovereignty of multiple sources of data does also.

HOW SHOULD A DISASTER GO? EVENTS AND THEIR NARRATIVES

How should a fire go? How long does a fire burn? How long should a fire last? What is a good fire and a bad fire? An earthquake, a flood, a tornado, a bombing, a war? What is the "unit" of trauma? Who all are affected? How do we know? How do individuals, families, and large groups structure and punctuate catastrophes in time? Of all the terrible things that happen to people, how is it that some events come to be selected or chosen (Volkan, 1991) for inter-generational memory, and others are "metabolized"? When disaster occurs, what leads to resilience, and what leads to paralysis? What is the relationship between the "objective" and the "subjective" facets of disaster? That is, disaster both *happens to* people and to culture (in the abstract sense) and *occurs within* the membrane of people's (including group's) lives. Catastrophe is both outside and inside. We need to examine both what people *bring to* disaster and what the disaster *induces* or *unleashes*. This is the dual face and paradox of disaster.

Hardly has a disaster begun than it takes shape in some recognizable aesthetic form, narrative and otherwise. Perhaps the form by which we account for and recount it even precedes a particular catastrophe. As if we were all cultural Platonists, we know an event before it happens: how it goes or should go, its outcome, who its protagonists are or should be. We even know how to recover or to try to recover before it happens. Disasters—how ever we come to define them—seem to be in our heads and in our cultural protocols prior to their appearance in the world.

In this study of learning from disaster, I say in many ways that despite our claims to learn from experience, we often do not. More often than not, we impose our narrative and ideological order on experience. For example, we herd people into crisis management debriefing sessions. Or, alternately, we descend on them with armies of grief counselors. Or alternately again, in public ceremony, we say a prayer, order the American flag raised to full mast, and declare the disaster to be over. Or again, we declare mourning to be for sissies, and tell ourselves and tell others that we should be glad we were not killed, and insist that everyone get back to work as if nothing had happened. Each approach is highly rationalized, culturally, even scientifically.

What goes omitted is that there are *many* earthquakes and fires even in "the same" one, not only a single one, and that many people are omitted (and exclude themselves) from assistance, or too many are included in assistance, or they are given the wrong assistance. Formulas and protocols replace personal experience. The formulas and protocols come to define and prescribe experience. Often, our healing rituals not only protect us; they imprison us and teach us to fool ourselves. We thereby avoid the disorganizing anxiety that is at the root of psychological catastrophe. The process becomes an even more closed system when the healers or counselors avoid their own anxiety through treatment of clients and communities.

To state the point again, things are not what they seem. Disasters, we say, are terrible, unwelcome events in the communities on which they wreak so much destruction. Yet, during the people of rescue, recovery, and rebuilding, there emerges a camaraderie, a feeling of brotherhood and sisterhood, and an open expression of feelings that are all but absent during ordinary times. Even as the destruction to community is mourned, a sense of community erupts in the midst of the rubble. Often, when a disaster is "over," at least officially, many participants look back longingly to the sense of closeness and connectedness people had back then. Even in the midst of calamity, people sense that the intimacy and generosity will come to an end.

They ask: How long can we sustain the feelings, or how can we get them back?

Terrible as disasters are, the relationships that emerge during them feel more real than life. In addition to the disaster "proper," these intense temporary relationships, too, eventually are over and must be mourned. If disasters are often experienced as desecrations to property and to life, the work in their midst is often felt to be sacred—a kind of consecration. Disasters are *symbols* as much as they are terrible events. They are imbued with significance we cannot know without inquiring.

Can we tolerate to learn as we go, or do we require finished formulas, airtight mass disaster planning, beforehand? Can we ever be completely prepared for the next disaster? Is, perhaps, the wish to be totally prepared for the next time, in part a response to having been caught unprepared, vulnerable, feeling helpless before—in short, an effort, via repetition, to correct the past in the future?

WHAT ARE WE TALKING ABOUT? DISASTER, LANGUAGE, MEANING, FEELING, POWER, AND FIDELITY

This chapter is about remembering, understanding, and helping in relation to events—however defined—in which people feel their worlds ripped apart. It is about social groups we call communities, about people who label themselves "us," and about the labeling of others as "them." For example, it is about the word "healing" as it applies to all sorts of people afflicted by the event, "touched" by the event: people we variously label as victims, casualties, survivors, rescuers, healers. It is about healing the healers as well as those whom healers help. It is about categories and words, and about what these words mean and omit.

In fact, many people detest the very word "healers" and "healing"! They bring to a fire and to other disasters other images, experiences, and languages. So we must not even take the "what" for granted. This chapter is thus about the multiplicity of viewpoints and experiences in relation to the "same" event we call disaster or catastrophe. It is about language, what language includes and excludes. It begins with the approach of the first anniversary of a fire that killed six firefighters in Worcester, Massachusetts, and that shook a community—any communities and senses of community—as much as any earthquake could.

Whatever else this chapter is about, it is also about the issue of *fidelity* in relation to understanding and helping in disasters or catastrophes (Apprey, 2000). Oddly perhaps, many of us—researchers, clinicians, healers—are more faithful to theory, method, and technique than we are to the phenomenon itself and to the people afflicted with it, ourselves included (Devereux, 1967; Boyer, 1999; Stein, 2000). Our words get in the way of the very process of understanding, even as we must use words to help us to understand. Conceptually and perceptually, it is hard to know what is cultural *prism* and what is *prison*.

In families—however broadly we choose to define *that* unit (see La Barre, 1954)—all members do not go through the "stages" in the identical sequence or have the same "rates" or "timetables" for mourning. Even though "the same" person died, each person in the family, or each grouping of people in the family, has lost a "different" person, due to a host of factors: age, how long the person had been known, the nature of the relationship, etc. In certain respects, it is no different in nations and in large cultures. Not only do some individuals "process" an event differently from others, but groups "process" the event differently from one another. Losses reactivate earlier losses, and characteristic defenses against them. Further, in mass disasters, some may lose people and places they know *personally*, while others may experience these losses as *public symbols* (symbolic objects), that is, primarily if not exclusively through projecting and identifying, as representations.

The larger the symbolic magnitude and burden of the event—political assassinations, military defeats, bombings, fires, weather catastrophes—the broader the sense of loss, whether of people or of place. The federal building in Oklahoma City was a place where many people throughout Oklahoma had been or might have been if they had had business there at the time of the bombing. Many people throughout Oklahoma knew people who had been there or were related to them. Practically speaking, the federal building was an edifice that occupied the consciousness of many rather than of only a few; it represented an inclusive "us" and not an exclusive "them." The federal building was also a highly visible symbolic presence of the ambivalently-held federal government. Of all the categories of the 168 people who were killed in the bombing, greatest and most prolonged attention was paid to the children who died in the facility's day care center. Even in traumatic death, the deaths of some categories of people are ranked as more intolerable than others.

The Worcester Cold Storage, though long vacant, was nonetheless a massive monument-like structure in the downtown, one virtually everyone knew of and had been past. Other buildings, other deaths, and other survivors are often far less symbolized and are thus far less noticed—for instance, firefighters who died in less spectacular blazes, widows Korean War (often called "The Forgotten War") veterans, and Vietnam War veterans themselves. The consequences of symbolization and of its lack are a central issue in disaster response. We often lose these seemingly subtle, local distinctions, in our attempt to develop broadly applicable theories and methods of disaster response.

Consider but a few of the terms we use habitually now: stress, stressor, trauma, disaster, catastrophe, critical incident, post-traumatic stress disorder, critical incident stress management, debriefing, defusing, flashback, emergency response, healing, psychotherapy, crisis intervention, and so on. Many of us act as if these terms were self-evident, real, and universal. I know legions of people—and not only of Oklahoma culture—who insist that they not only do not have, but couldn't have, "stress," that only "wimps" or sissies (weak people) have stress, that if one is truly a Christian, one could not possibly have stress because one has strong faith instead. They are affronted if one insinuates that they are under "stress," even after a bombing or a tornado. (As an aside, I add that for these people, while it is anathema to have any "mental" illness, "physical" illness is acceptable and preferred.) Although the work of comprehending and helping following a disaster is not limited to people's proclaimed language, it is a place respectfully to begin. Fidelity to the phenomenon and to the people who are inseparable from its influence helps us to hone theory, method, and technique. The first vignette illustrates both the difficulty of maintaining this fidelity and the depth of understanding that occurs when this faith is kept.

Vignette 1: A Vignette from the Worcester Institute Planning Committee Meeting

My first extended vignette consists of an example from a meeting of the planning committee for the Worcester conference at which this chapter was presented. It turns out that this planning committee is not only a decision-making body, but also a microcosm of group processes ranging from Worcester to the USA. About ten of us had a weekly, and later, monthly, lunch meeting or visit, one of which occurred on May 25, 2000, for about an hour and fifteen minutes. I was "present" long-distance via a telephone placed on the conference table—between the chicken salad and yogurt, specifically—as committee member Marjorie Cahn later told me in an e-mail message. We discussed speakers, topics, workshops, and sequence. Nearly an hour through the meeting, someone noticed that in the entire planning thus far, the fire itself had not been explicitly, directly mentioned – something that occurred in earlier meetings as well. Another person wondered where we should bring it up, how we should bring it up at the conference: "The fire, NOT the fire, where do we put it?"

From my distant office in Oklahoma City, I said that I had the fantasy, similar to that in families of alcoholics or drug addicts, that there is this giant elephant in the middle of the table. Everyone knows it is there; yet it is too emotionally enormous, taboo, to talk about, *even among us*. Now, here, in Worcester, what's in the middle of the table is the fire, far more dangerous, consuming, than a mere elephant. Someone brought up the issue of communication at the conference: How do we talk about bad events? On the one hand, we try to avoid them—speaking, for example, only about courage and the wish to get the fire behind us; on the other hand, we hyperbolize about the fire. I said that my fantasy, and perhaps our fear, is of being consumed by the fire. It is very hard to put a fire anywhere, even the subject of fire. Maybe we were identifying with it as a way of trying to control it.

As we were approaching the end of our meeting, someone brought up the issue of a "wrap-up" of the conference at the end, on the subject of communication and synthesis. Another person then mentioned coffee and tea, evaluations and continuing education presentations, and said that the wrap-up is "not a nuclear melt-down," an even more violent image of the fire. I said something to the effect that it was important for us, the planners, to track our own imagery and feelings, because they are mirrors of the kinds of metaphors and emotions that are, and will be, percolating throughout Worcester and far beyond. As the planning committee, we not only must deal with our resistance to the event that prompted the conference, but with our planning committee's process is part of the conference. In plain English: This is how people, including professional people, including people of very good will, deal with the fire and with its equivalents in other places. We struggle to understand; the struggle is part of the understanding. Helpers of all professions can be deeply and unconsciously affected by a disaster, and thus not even recognize its presence until it is *enacted* in some way.

I cannot help but speculate further that the attempt to place "me" (via the telephone) on the conference table was symbolic, as well as practical: a kind of condensation of the wish to have me present (person, nutrient) against the backdrop of enormous loss and grief. When we talk about gathering data about the fire, some of the most crucial data we can "gather" is not only from "them," but also from "us." Ultimately, fidelity to genuine healing begins with fidelity to the catastrophe itself and to people's experiences and accounts. Part of that fidelity is to the observer, clinician, or consultant's own emotional response, that is, to one's countertransference.

TRAUMATIZATION AND VICTIMIZATION: OR, WHAT'S IN A WORD?

A formulation of Frank M. Ochberg (1997), one of the early formulators of the controversial concept of the "Post-Traumatic Stress Disorder" (PTSD), is especially enlightening in the understanding of the Worcester fire and any calamity.

> There is a considerable difference between the impact of human cruelty, a particular form of trauma, which I call, arbitrarily, "victimization," and natural or accidental events. The generic term for any catastrophic encounter, including earthquake, fire and flood, is, by contrast, "traumatization." When we defined PTSD, we ignored this difference. PTSD was traumatization. But every "victimized" patient of mine complains less about "traumatization" than about "victimization." What are the symptoms of victimization? These include shame, self-blame, feeling lowered in dominance, disgust, paradoxical gratitude (the Stockholm Syndrome), and other stigmata of encounters with evil (see Ochberg, 1988). Victims of cruelty are not just terrified by death and destruction—they are dehumanized and belittled. Primo Levi used the expression "to lie on the bottom" to explain how he and

> his fellow concentration camp victims were diminished. In some respects, dehumanization is worse than death. Death is biological. Dehumanization is spiritual.
>
> [W]e should attend to assaults on spirit, as opposed to assaults on flesh. We need, in my opinion, to explore the human response to cruelty, because forms of endurance and adaptation perpetuate cruelty. Silence may be merely diminished oxygenation of grey matter. Silence may be unexpressed shame. Silence may be the price of survival in a totalitarian state or a totalitarian family. (pp. 202-203)

Now, I do not want to overdraw Ochberg's typological distinction between "natural" and "human" assaults and make them polar opposites. In a similar vein, Volkan (2000) argues that "A closer look suggests that it is sometimes difficult to discriminate between different types of disasters" (p. 3). For example, North American prairie grain (wheat, milo, corn) farmers whose fields are devastated by severe weather, and who are certainly traumatized by storm, flood, tornado, hail, and drought, also highly personalize (anthropomorphize) the destructive event. Further, they often feel a sense of guilt, shame, and blame for some dimly-recollected wrong-doing, as though a "natural" disaster were punishment by divine forces. Traumatization can be experienced *as* victimization. A personalized, anthropomorphized Nature, even God, can feel cruel. Further, "bad" weather can be blamed on "bad" government and on "bad" cities, as if even natural disasters can be deliberately caused.

Consider a related example: During the summer of 2000, a fire raged in and around the Mesa Verde National Park. When the Ute Mountain Ute Indians look eastward to the national park, many do not simply see a natural disaster. "They see spirits that are mad—blazing mad," reporter Nancy Lofholm writes (2000, p.7A). Lofholm quotes Terry Knight, spiritual leader of the Ute: "'The old spirits that are there are not at rest. Their energy is off-balance, and this causes things to happen in the metaphysical world. … There is something happening with that tribe within the ground. These spirits are getting back at people for doing this and that'" (2000, p. 7A). Anger is directed both toward the white man and toward Indians for various metaphysical violations, such as disturbing Indian remains and storing them in museums.

In many Utes' experience of the prolonged, devastating fire, the cataclysm is personal, not purely natural; it is retaliation for peoples' unexpiated guilt and shame. More broadly, the experience of being the intended target or victim of hurt seems to be of critical psychological importance in influencing the course of responding to any disaster or trauma. What we might regard as "pure" trauma, others might imbue with the quality of victimization—induced by one's own group and/or by others. If some of our clinical and managerial categories illumine, reveal, they also obscure, conceal. PTSD and CISD must be included among them (see Young, 1996). Things are not what they seem.

"THE REST OF THE STORY"—OR AT LEAST MORE OF IT: WHO IS AFFECTED BY TRAUMA?

Throughout this project I take the radio editorialist Paul Harvey's approach or methodology of noting the conventional, if not official, obligatory, story, and exploring more of it, if not "the rest of the story." I ask the reader to do so likewise, in the spirit of earnest play. I say repeatedly: Things are not what they seem, what we want them to seem, even what we insist that they are. If your terms, our language, help us to help others and ourselves in times of cataclysm, our language also gets in the way. Notions of *healing, intervention, closure, faith,* and *resilience* can wound and impede healing as much as they can help it.

For instance, the view of *time* is part of the solution and the problem created by catastrophe. Timetables of healing, individual, family, organizational, and community, can sometimes artificially foreclose or prolong the process of healing. Timetables can become inner and group deadlines, achievement scales, which prescribe when something should be finished, completed, and which add to guilt, shame, anxiety, and isolation, when the "outcome" is not attained.

Who—who all—are "affected" by a disaster (see Silver et. al., 2002)? What "units" or "categories" of people are included in, and excluded from, consideration? Who is recognized, and who passes (and is isolated, perhaps self-isolated) as unrecognized and overlooked? What is the geographic and temporal compass or scope of the event? Who should be taken seriously as affected by it? Who merits empathy? When we think in terms of cultural *units*, we likely think in terms of ethnic group, religion, and nationality. Yet workplaces and work roles (occupations, professions, jobs) are often units of affiliation and belonging: for instance, the firehouse, the fire department, the police department, the company, the corporation. Traditionally, at least, the men in a fire station lived and functioned and "bonded" as a family. When loss occurs, members of other cultures—ethnic, national, religious, occupational—might not comprehend the depth of the sense of loss.

In Oklahoma after the 1995 bombing, three categories of people were quickly identified (created) and then reified: "those killed" (the victims), "those who survived," and "those who were forever changed." Who is a "survivor" or "victim" of a catastrophe? Who is "forever changed?" Following the Oklahoma City bombing, firefighters were publicly honored, but in large measure many police and nurses felt left out, overlooked, as if nothing catastrophic had happened to them, as though their own efforts had been less than heroic. Who, we must ask, *deserves* to be considered as affected by the disaster? Are not all "helpers" of the first-line "helpers" themselves at least potential casualties of their attempt to hold onto and process experiences that are unbearable (often called "secondary traumatization")? To complicate matters further, not all people will be "affected" at the same time—a view of a disaster's "effect" that differs from the official one. If it is widely accepted that all pragmatics contains an implicit ethics, often the official ethics omits many people and categories of people from its compass.

My experience has been much like that of the colleague mentioned at the beginning of this chapter. Months, even years, after the Oklahoma City bombing, I will visit a clinic or give a talk to a clinical group, and the subject of the bombing will come up. I will ask the doctor or nurse, or a spouse of a health caregiver, about the "effect" of the bombing for them, and suddenly tears will flow. The person will often say: "No one asked me before what it was like. They just told us to get back to work and be glad we had a job. Or, they'd say: 'What are you whining about? You weren't the ones killed.' The inward- and outward-enforced delay is part of the depth of the catharsis. This raises the further question: Whose disaster is it? To whom does it belong? Who merits listening to, or intervention of some kind? Who has the power to do the including, the excluding, and the defining?

POWER AND THE CONSTRUCTION OF DISASTER

Consider, for instance, the widely used emergency management language of the Jeffrey Mitchell International Institute. When Mitchell (1996) says, "CISD [Critical Incident Stress Debriefing] is structure, order, the antidote to chaos", what do the words mean, what are their relationships, what is presupposed about order and chaos? When we speak of "critical incident management," what precisely makes an incident critical? To whom is the event critical? Who possesses or is imbued with the power to define the event? Whose event is it? When an event occurs, what are its boundaries in time, space, and person? Who is counted and who is discounted as critically affected? Who has the power to define eventfulness? How much of a critical event is the psychophysical property of the raw event itself, and how much is the property of projection, perception, and meaning (La Barre, 1971, 1972)? What is inherent to the event, and what is imposed so as to become definitional of the event itself?

In a classic study of a West Coast U.S. fire in a Samoan church, Ablon (1973) showed how different Samoan-American long term responses to the fire were in comparison with those of mainstream Whites to similar fires (e.g., the 1942 Coconut Grove fire). Differing family and community support systems, and differing body aesthetics distinguished responses to what was outwardly the same type of disaster. It is not so much that we have more questions than answers, but that we must take care not to neglect local community and cultural particulars when we attempt to make sweeping generalizations, such as the "effect" of disaster on culture and community.

How can we humans truly "manage" or control experiences that are felt as overwhelming the normal range of human experience? What assumptions do we make about what constitutes a "normal range"? And who is empowered to define what is and what is not overwhelming? What is the role of culture(s)—ethnic, national, local, community, professional, organizational—in this process of definition, inclusion, and exclusion? What about wars and civil wars, persecutions, expulsions, which take place for years, if not for decades? What happens to people when these become included within the realm of the ordinary, if not the normal? "Critical Incident Stress Debriefing" and "Management" have a distinctively American cultural ring or connotation to them in their emphasis on the causality of the external event, the decisiveness and brevity of the emergency response, the standardization and bureaucratization of response, and the expectation of rapid recovery. The logic of "crisis intervention" has little room for long-range planning or long-lasting suffering from loss. There is also the homogenizing assumption that one language fits all.

Clearly, all languages are not created equal: some are accorded more power, status, and funding than others. What and whose language(s) should we use? Does healing require that all participants agree to the same language (e.g., therapy, closure, debriefing,etc.) When we are dealing with human suffering, it is the suffering, spoken and unspoken, that should occupy the center, not the languages we are most comfortable with in translation. Yet, political factors such as power, authority, public symbolism and meaning, and professional stature all affect the response to suffering.

What, for instance, is the relationship between *disaster* (or cognate terms) and their *narratives*, between disaster narratives and experience (Frank 2000; Mattingly 1998)? What do people bring to disasters, and what do people make of and take away from disasters? What do we—and who all are the "we"—think a disaster looks, sounds, feels, and smells like? What constitutes the "scene" or occupies the "front stage" of a disaster? What is relegated to the "wings" or the "backstage"?

What disaster accounts or stories become public, and what ones are kept or relegated to secret or private? What is the human cost of a psychological splitting of people into acknowledgeable public ideals—containers of popular wish—and unacknowledgeable private shame? What kind of help is helpful? A trauma industry, like an alcoholism and drug abuse industry, now flourishes. How does one distinguish between opportunity and opportunism? These questions, if also "academic" or "intellectual," are dire ones: how we answer them directs us to what we will do and not do, whom we will consider and not consider.

Whom do we "treat" or conduct "emergency interventions" with? What and who are a "victim" or "survivor" (etc.) of disaster? What helps to rebuild inner and outer worlds destroyed? What happens to the grief at the flashpoint of loss in times of disaster? What is "its" story, not only the story of the calamity itself? How does making sense of what happened "here" (e.g.,

Worcester) help in the understanding, rebuilding, and disaster planning for what happened and will happen elsewhere? And, the reverse as well: how can the comparative method of understanding adaptation to disaster helps us in our own disaster?

To understand a group's conception of disaster and of preparedness, one must understand the philosophy behind, say, its "strategic planning" (or its lack), and the theology behind what is included in (and excluded from) the "procedures manuals" and SOPs (standard operating procedures), and the cultural equivalents. One must know about technological and logistical matters, but also about much more. One must be willing to learn what many people do not want to know—including a society's gatekeepers of healing.

The test of whether a given clinician's "therapeutic emplotment" (Mattingly, 1998) is therapeutic or anti-therapeutic depends on whether the clinical strategy and clinical ideology serve as an "automatic" defense against anxiety (Devereux, 1967) and thus assure ignorance and emotional anaesthesia in both therapist and client, and wider. Here, culture—as a systematization of thought—can both help and hinder the healing process (or whatever other term one prefers to call it). Certain clinical narratives and therapeutic emplotments are culturally empowered, if not enforced. That is, they receive their authority and power by the abnegation of critical thinking and the ceding of judgment to the imagined omniscience of other, "higher" authorities (Boyer, 1999, pp. 103-112). Some clinical ideologies and methods achieve their effect by first re-traumatizing the very clients or patients to whom their practitioners are offering help. By the coercive and exclusive power ascribed to some clinical narratives and therapeutic emplotments, "outcome" measures are highly circumscribed and prescribed, and in turn become "proof" of the truthfulness of the narrative and ritual form. If surprise in the patient and client alike is essential to healing, it is also the element most often excluded from healing—ranging from individual conflict to collective disaster.

MEANING AND DISASTER: FROM CONCRETENESS TO CULTURAL PHILOSOPHY AND ITS EMERGENCE

To understand a group's—or many groups'—response to disaster, one must learn—more indirectly than directly—what they are afraid of and what they are not. To understand what a group is prepared and unprepared for, one must ask how they see themselves in relation to the cosmos, in relation to time, in relation to causality (including will), and in relation to responsibility. To understand a group's concepts of disaster and preparedness, one must understand their conception of their relationship to nature, to time, to agency (e.g., being, becoming, doing) (Kluckhohn and Strodtbeck, 1961).

For example, to understand how a group "fights" fires, one must know what they "fight" and to what they submit or yield. One must know what meanings and feelings and fantasies and fascinations fire holds for them—and for their wider constituency. For the most part, these *emerge* over time and are not present or stated from the outset. A disaster may be deeply meaning-ful and feeling-ful to people other than those whom we regard culturally as "directly affected." Among many people, there are at least three injuries: the original one, from the disaster itself; from the significance of the disaster; and from others' response to the disaster. Neglect of and indifference to people affected by a disaster lead to subsequent narcissistic hurt and to the development of a sense of entitlement—or, alternately, non-entitlement. As if the original disaster were not damaging enough, there often emerge issues of justice and injustice with respect to whether one's experience was acknowledged. "Grief" and "grievance" share a common sense of *loss*.

The experience of loss and of widespread public recognition in one group often triggers identification among related and even seemingly unrelated groups. It unleashes the sense of vulnerability, the memory of suffering, and the claim of entitlement if not the demand for restitution. Public recognition of one group triggers a sense of narcissistic injury and the protest of injustice in other groups. It is as if to say: "What about us? We suffered too." Still others, differently defended, will respond less with regression and narcissistic demands, as much as they will with reaction formation, as if to say, "We (or they) suffered too, but we moved on with our lives." More generally speaking, *the loss from the current disaster will trigger or rekindle memories and feelings associated with losses often far removed in time from the current event*. We will only take notice of, and try to understand, these subsequent unfoldings if we can accept that things are not what they seem. This is all part of the "fidelity" of which I speak. I illustrate this with a second extended vignette.

Vignette 2: The Retreat with the F-5 Game Plan

My second vignette comes from a medical department's faculty retreat, the goal of which was to foster group coherence via several small- and large-group exercises, such as designing the first page of a newspaper that would have headlines, pictures, sidebars, and stories depicting the department's imagined future. The date was May 7, 1999. The retreat was held at a pastoral conference center in Oklahoma City. As we worked, we could see the lovely, quiet spring day through the gigantic picture windows. As we went through our various groups and tasks, I wondered what all the retreat was about.

In my own small group, through energetic participation, we developed an image of the Medical Center arising, phoenix-like, out of the rubble of the collapse and ruins of downsizing, restructuring, hospitals, managed care, and national health. Debris everywhere surrounded the stately columns marked "education, service, and research" that stood out from the destruction. In a subsequent large group, several people commented that we needed the force of a tornado to achieve our goals; that we required a total flattening of the organization to make things work; that the debris from all this change is in Kansas (an allusion to the movie, *The Wizard of Oz*); and that we were going in so many directions as a department that we needed "The Force" to be with us to accomplish our avowed goals (an allusion to the *Star Wars* movie series, in which "The Force" was a great benevolent power on the side of goodness). One person spoke of "The ivory tower scattered like a tornado." One group offered a bold new idea for clinics' reorganization at the end of the day. Images of major reconstruction alternated with images of massive destruction. At the end of the day-long retreat, we named the departmental plan for the future "The F-5 Game Plan."

Four days earlier, on May 3, 1999, a series of deadly tornadoes ripped through central Oklahoma, killing twenty-five people and destroying over a thousand homes. The path of one of the tornadoes lay only a couple of miles away from the idyllic site of the retreat. Whatever else the departmental retreat was officially "about," it was also about the reverberation of the catastrophe in the emotional life of an organizational group. Outside had become inside, variously energizing, terrifying, organizing and disorganizing. One could offer a variety of interpretations—beginning with the most obvious, identification with the (anthropomorphized) aggressor. However, my present point for introducing the vignette is to describe and evoke how *psychologically* present a disaster can become, how it can influence the *work* of a group – and the group be oblivious to the very catastrophic psychology it is enacting. Having first been a terrifying *reality*, the tornado became a personal and group psychological *representation*, a presence that may have fused both fear and wish with respect to aggressiveness.

Fidelity to people's experiences—including experiences that are enacted and articulated as symbols—can take us to the heart of a disaster and to cues as to how to be of help. If one is going to "fight" fires (military, war metaphor), one must learn something not only about firefighting, but also about the phenomenology and meaning of fire itself (see Bachelard, 1964). The same holds for tornadoes, hurricanes, bombings, floods, and wars. It is not accidental that competitive sports teams often name themselves for hurricanes, tornadoes, and other fierce forces of nature (and human as well) that strike a region. Through identification, team members hope to strike—and win—with the ferocity of "mother" and "father" Nature.

DISASTER AND ITS MANY DAMAGES: PLACE AND SENSE OF PLACE

Any assessment of the "damage" or destruction a catastrophe causes or unleashes must be made both from the outside and the inside (what anthropologists-linguists call "etic" and "emic" perspectives respectively). Such points of view, both inside and outside, are numerous and not at all self-evident. There are the official measures such as loss of life, injury, loss of property, loss of productivity, and the like. There is often also damage to the (anthropomorphized) group psyche, to the collective self-image, to the "tissue" or "fabric" (K. Erikson, 1976; Rangell, 1976) of a community—which is to say, to those networks without which massive separation anxiety is unleashed.

Consider how one compensates—and feels compelled to compensate—for one's (reified) place and sense of place when, through a disaster, the projected place-image and its associated group self-image comes up tarnished. I think of Dallas, Texas, in the shadow of President Kennedy's November 22, 1963 assassination; or of Galveston, Texas, in the wake of the September 8, 1900, hurricane that swept over the island and killed 6,000 people and left another 10,000 homeless; or of Hartford, Connecticut, whose Barnum and Bailey circus tent, waterproofed by paraffin and gasoline, caught fire and consumed 167 people on July 6, 1944. The death of 118 Russian sailors during late August 2000 on the flagship nuclear submarine *Kursk* received world shock and grief, while the Russian army felt its thousands of dead neglected and forgotten in the still-popular war against separatist Chechnya.

Grief, resilience, and recovery are made more complicated the more a group's identity and self-image prior to the disaster is bound up with shame or pride—e.g., the Russian government's reluctance to ask for international help as soon as their submarine was in trouble. Galveston, Texas, was the self-proclaimed "Queen of the Gulf [of Mexico]" in the years before the hurricane for which it was so neglectfully unprepared. Hubris and shame are part of the damage. The sorrow and publicity around the September 1, 2000 deaths of two Oklahoma officers—an Oklahoma City policeman and a highway patrolman—during a high speed automobile chase is linked at least in part with the lack of public acknowledgment the police received and felt after the 1995 bombing, especially in comparison with the adulation feted on the firefighters. The assessment of material damage to a *place* is inseparable from the assessment of the damage to the *sense of place* (which dislocations include separation anxiety that interrupts the fantasy of merger with an idealized maternal object). Place symbolism (together with identity and role symbolism) deserves to be part of the "damage assessment" in any calamity.

Disaster is rarely, if ever, a purely objective, physical event. It is invested and imbued with meaning, symbolism, and emotion. Is the scale of death on the ocean liner Titanic even thinkable apart from the audacity, if not hubris, with which the ship was launched and set sail? Are not the self-image and national image of the mythical American "Heartland"—innocence, "true grit," virtue—and its violation intrinsic to the experience of the 1995 bombing of the federal building in Oklahoma City? One can almost propose a "formula," to the effect that, the greater the symbolic, meaning-ful, and emotional burden of a cataclysm, the more its mourning and recovery will be complicated by defensive, narcissistic dynamic in individual, family, community, and culture. Military defeats, losses of land and property, that are bound up with childhood trauma and conflict, often cannot be mourned. They become internally encapsulated, transmitted to subsequent generations for restitution, revenge, and repair. What cannot be mourned will be repeated (Volkan, 1988, 1997). This "complicated" reaction to loss averts the disorganizing experience of grief. It manifests itself through blame, through lawsuits, and other action against a world experienced as "bad" and persecutory (Fornari, 1966/1975). Individuals, families, communities, and whole national cultures that cannot let go of a loss will find some way to restage it—in some kind of "war" or "sacrifice." This is an especially good reason to make sure no one following a disaster is overlooked, discounted, or allowed to "slip through the cracks," so as to help prevent malignant narcissism from growing under the scab of the wound.

My third vignette shows how a potentially complicated grieving was averted through early, perhaps fortuitous, attention to symbol, meaning, and feeling.

Vignette 3: Outer and Inner Catastrophes:
A Vignette from the May 3, 1999, Great Plains Tornado

My third vignette comes from Oklahoma City. Two days after the May 3rd tornado, I was in the process of leaving a meeting in a clinical department. As everyone else was quickly leaving, a senior physician with whom I had worked for nearly two decades approached me. The meeting had been uneventful and had been like similar ones I had attended. As he came closer, I noticed that his eyes were very red. He looked exhausted. He said to me: "You're kind of in the psychological field. Is it normal for a man to get tearful after a tornado rips through your town? I'm teary all the time. Will they stop? What am I asking you for? I know what you'll say. But I've never had feelings as intense as this. I'm a physician and a specialist in workplace catastrophes, so there ain't much I haven't seen. I don't know why I keep getting tearful. It's embarrassing. It comes over me in waves."

I stumbled to say *something* to a man I deeply respected as a scientist, physician, pathologist, and toxicologist in occupational medicine. My family and I had crouched low in our bathtub on the night of May 3. I think I just asked him to "Tell me what's going on. You look exhausted"—a look different from what I had ever seen of this spry, usual witty, man in his sixties. He continued, saying something like:

> I spent all night down in Moore, Oklahoma [one of the heavily populated areas hardest hit by the F-5 tornado]. That was on top of my regular job. I was trying to help people sort through the rubble of their homes, to help people fill out insurance forms and file insurance claims, trying to do anything that might be helpful. I saw all these people out in the streets looking back at heaps that had been their homes. It was unreal. I was spooked. This one fellow started pacing back and forth near the curb that had his house number on it. His house was completely gone. It looked almost like a vacant lot. What was someone supposed to do to help him?

> I put my arm around his shoulder and just stood there with him. The world had been taken away, and all I could do was paperwork to help folks remember what they had.

He continued speaking for several minutes, relating incident after incident from that night, as if he were trying to put together broken glass. He described the eerie sight at shelters where he had seen people standing vigil over their few possessions. They wouldn't let them out of their sight. He returned to the theme of not understanding why he is so *emotional* about this, why he can't get it out of his mind, why he can't let go of the images of the rubble. I thought to ask him about the rubble, what he "saw" in it, but I didn't want to bombard him with questions. Instead, I listened to him via listening to myself, so to speak. I sensed that he needed to tell someone who would listen, someone who would hold onto the story as it was coming to him, and to help him make sense of it.

As he spoke, my thoughts and feelings entered a surreal "twilight zone" that collapsed space and time. I remembered that he had been an early "responder" at the scene of the bombing of the Murrah Federal Building in downtown Oklahoma City four years earlier. I wondered aloud whether there might be some connection between the tornado and the bombing. He said that it was an interesting idea, one that he'd never thought of. We visited for a few more minutes. As we parted, I told him that I appreciated that he was comfortable talking with me about this difficult subject, and that I wanted him to know that I was available to talk with him any time—even by phone at night if he needed it. He thanked me.

About a week later, we were at a similar clinical meeting. After it was over, my friend approached me. He looked tired, but very much like himself rather than someone haunted. I asked him how he was doing. He said:

> I'm doing much better. I want to tell you how much I appreciate our visit last week, and to tell you that something you said helped me to figure out what was going on that had made me so emotional, so volatile. You provided the trigger, the missing piece: the bombing. You asked me whether there was any connection between the tornado and the bombing. It got me to thinking: What bothered me *most* about all the devastation after the tornado was that I kept seeing all this blackened stuff in the rubble. I tried to avoid looking. [He was speaking now in a different "voice," as if in a kind of trance, re-living something.] I got to thinking: I remember where I saw this before. I was one of the people the authorities had go through what was left of the Murrah Building less than twenty-four hours after the bombing to determine where it was safe to go. This was even before a lot of the rescuers and recovery personnel were inside. The police wanted to know what we were dealing with toxicologically. What kinds of solvents, or explosives, were around that the rescuers and fireman might be

> exposed to? So they had me walk around in stuff where no one had been yet.

He paused, then continued:

> As I was looking for possible exposures, I kept seeing blackened body parts, blackened blood on body parts. I don't remember looking directly at them. It's like I didn't want to see it but I saw it anyway. I couldn't help but see them. Nobody should have to see sights like that, burned bones poking through metal and stone. *That's* what was so overwhelming when I was helping out after the tornado. It was a *flashback*! I'd never had them before. I thought I saw the same thing again. I couldn't be sure, just as I didn't look closely enough in the Murrah Building to say for positive that charred flesh and bones are what I saw. But I didn't want to see it again.

As he told the latter part of the story, my abdomen tightened; I began to feel nausea. I trust my countertransference, my emotional response, to have conveyed the revulsion he had experienced. I do not know whether there was in him a forbidden wish behind the revulsion, but I sensed the disgust and horror. He thanked me for helping him to "piece together" what had happened and to help him understand why the tornado had had such an emotional effect on him. If he felt understood, I also felt understood, capable of understanding, capable—at least then—of *bearing* to hold on to not-knowing, able to accompany him in discovering more of the story. He became re-connected to the "more" that overwhelmed him. One could speculate that he had dissociated the experience into an alter-self or ego-alien fragment, but what is most crucial is the phenomenology, and the relationship that permits the phenomenology to emerge, and for healing to occur.

My colleague and friend can be considered to have been a "direct" helper and early responder following both the 1995 Oklahoma City bombing and the 1999 central Oklahoma tornado. My role was more indirect, more unofficial. I brought to our visit multiple conceptual viewpoints, ranging from a psychoanalytic developmental one to a cross-cultural comparison of trauma. Most of all, I sought to suspend these and listen to him, and not listen primarily through the defensive use of theory and method. He, together with the emotions, fantasies, and body sensations that our discussion engendered in me by projective identification, led me to "provide" what he needed (Boyer, 1999).

TRANSFERENCE, PLACE SYMBOLISM, AND DISASTER

Much of the memory, symbolism, and emotion linked to a disaster can be understood through the concepts of "transference objects" or "transference targets." Cataclysms do not occur in value vacuums; they do not just "happen" neutrally. They are assigned meaning, often before they occur. These objects and targets—ranging from persons, to groups, to places—can be focus of "positive transference," that is, overestimation and idealization, or of "negative transference," that is, hatred or demonization. In either case, one is unconsciously "transferring" to them, projecting on them, feelings and images that originated in an earlier relationship, often one from childhood.

A few brief examples will illustrate this process. In the contemporary U.S., the popular response to the idea of, and attitudes toward, firefighters is inseparable from the "positive transference," while the response to the idea of, and attitudes toward, postal workers and the U.S. Post Office, is inseparable from the "negative transference." Put differently, the image of the firefighter is of the generous, kindly, self-sacrificial, parental rescuer, while that of the postal worker is of the disturbed person who might suddenly "go postal," as the popular expression holds, and massacre people. The firefighter occupies the image of the "good parent," and the postal worker occupies the image of the "bad parent." Cultural myth—which may be informally and officially exploited—makes some people greater than life and others less than life. Some people are more than human, while others are less than human. Here, reality is not somewhere "in the middle," but is overridden entirely. Heroes can do no wrong, and villains can do no right. Through stereotypes—positive and negative alike—we claim to know people without ever meeting them. Stereotypes become further compounded by wider social reality. For instance, in today's steeply competitive and privatism-ridden America, firefighters are one of the increasingly rare groups dedicated unabashedly to the public good.

Positive and negative stereotypes, and the transferences behind them, hold everyone hostage to fixed images. For instance, benevolent and heroic acts by police have a hard time combating the popular image of the policeman (or –woman) who gives you a speeding ticket, who arrests you for doing something you wished to do but at which you instead were caught. The policeman prevents you from doing something, or punishes you for having done it. In many cases, police represent our own projected guilty consciences, our own sadism, and our own prohibiting and punishing parents. Fire trucks are more often children's toys than police cars. Firefighters are perceived to be unambivalent, while police are viewed more suspiciously as "political." Firefighters are seen as good-to-all, while police are seen as partial to some members of ethnic groups and heavy-handed to others. Firefighters are also more "experience-near" public safety officials than police, bringing fire trucks into residential communities and letting children climb all over them.

To cite another example, homeless people, who are often fused with people who are chronically mentally ill, have an almost anti-hero image. In a productivity-driven and independence-espousing culture, they are seen as embodying sloth and dependency. They, like firefighters, postal workers, and police, are what La Barre (1946) called "social cynosures," categories of people who attract a lot of attention. Homeless people who are culturally recruited to contain unwanted or unattainable part of ourselves.

Through these socially held transferences, we claim to "know" people whom we have never met. When disaster strikes "good" people and places, public shock and grief are longer and more intense than when disaster strikes "bad" people and places. To the effect of this splitting must be added the complicating factor of unconscious ambivalence beneath firmly held "positions" of idealization and demonization, or at least disparagement. The hated villain may be secretly admired, while the admired hero may be secretly envied. Positive and negative group-held social transferences to persons, groups, and places help to shape the public response to their injury, damage, death, or destruction during disaster.

Further, in some cultures, people can be regarded as heroes only if they die for the cause and community they serve, that is, if they are "sacrifices." The term "sacrifice" was widely used to describe the heroism of the six Worcester firefighters who died on December 3, 1999. One wonders whether, when a term is so frequently used, there is a fantasy that the dead heroes are somehow community sacrifices as well as self-sacrifices. In the least, the image or stereotype of "sacrifice" adds to the idealizing transference.

The question *then* becomes when, under what circumstances, outer and inner, these stereotypes become forcefully applied and under what circumstances they are not. When does the emotional valency or power increase, and when does it diminish? In Oklahoma City, many members of the police force felt virtually left out of the public acknowledgment that was feted on the firefighters after the bombing. From my understanding of Worcester, Massachusetts, following the fire, there is a greater sense of fraternity, and shared recognition, between the two groups. One wonders what accounts for the differences, and what communities can learn from one another.

In Worcester, Massachusetts, the two homeless people who accidentally started the fire in the Worcester Cold Storage, and who left the building and did not report the fire, were sentenced only to five years of probation (*The Dallas Morning News*, 2002, p. 12A). In contrast to elsewhere, there seems to be widespread popular compassion in Worcester for homeless people. What accounts for the difference? What fosters healing, integration, instead of splitting, fragmentation? Perhaps local leadership is part of the explanation, e.g., the fire chief's decision to have firefighters enter the building as part of the definition of civic (and role) responsibility. Stereotypes play a large role in making categories of people larger than life or lesser than life. The issue is how, when, and why the stereotypes are applied and not applied.

To summarize: If catastrophe brings out the *best* in us, the most adaptive, it also brings out the *irrational* as well. In the fourth vignette, as in the third, the eruption of the irrational when it is least expected, comes to be recognized as a consequence of premature "resolution" or "closure."

Vignette 4: The Pain Beneath the Scab: From Non-Verbal to Verbal

My fourth vignette illustrates the cultural psychodynamics of Oklahomans around eight months after the bombing. Although it occurred in Oklahoma, the scenario might also be anywhere. To speak metaphorically, it reveals the levels or layers of meaning and feeling beneath a disaster many had thought to be now "behind us." It explores not only what emotionally takes place "beneath the surface," but also precisely the role that "surface" (the scab over the wound) plays in dynamic relation to what is beneath it. In early December, 1995, 1 was giving a talk to an Oklahoma mental health group on the long-term emotional consequences of the bombing. I had brought into the room and laid on the conference table a piece of granite from the Murrah Building.

One participant, a psychologist and pastoral counselor, continued to eye this artifact with misgiving long before I introduced it into my presentation. When I passed it around the room he pulled back, and handled it as if he were trying not to touch it. I asked him to help me to understand his intense discomfort, one I had labeled aloud as "anger." He assured me that he was surprised, not angry. Courageously, he continued to free associate to my presentation and to the unwelcome piece. He said he didn't want to hear about the bombing yet again, eight or nine months later. "The scab was healing," and here I came and picked it off. Then his voice softened, and his tense body relaxed.

> Maybe I need to feel what I don't want to feel. Maybe I still have strong feelings I haven't dealt with. Maybe I need to have the scab picked off and I'm afraid how much it will hurt. I look at that stone from the Murrah Building, and I'm thrown right back into April again. I hurt, but not as much as before. Maybe this time, the open wound will take less time to heal, and I'll heal more quickly.

Staying with his metaphor, we then briefly discussed two types of wound healing: from the top down, and from inside out. He had thought that he was healing properly from the top-down, now to discover that the authentic healing could only occur from the inside out. Between us was a moment of unimaginable grace. He said something generous like: "We keep helping each other. That is the best we can do." This case taught me the importance of interpersonal intimacy, the intersubjective fashioning of a "holding environment" (Winnicott, 1958, 1965) and "container" (Bion, 1956, 1957, 1977) in which the work of understanding, working through, and some healing could take place.

This vignette also illustrates the limits of externally and internally imposed *timetables* of when "closure" is supposed to occur, when grieving is expected to be "finished" or "over." From the viewpoint of theory and methodology, such seemingly universal (and universalized) terms such as "closure" and "completion" are cultural superimpositions (defenses) upon life in the guise of "natural" time. They reflect a condensation that extends from the intrapsychic realm to political agendas. The question of "When should it be over?" is culturally prescribed and ritualized, sometimes helpfully, sometimes hurtfully. In the absence of a respectful, compassionate holding environment, any "intervention" will be damaging in the guise of being helpful.

MEMORY AND MEMORIALS: DISASTER AND HOW WE REMEMBER

Perhaps the ultimate personal and group expression of "containing" and of "holding" the memory of disasters is a memorial space itself. Human groups of all kinds and sizes memorialize their victories and defeats, their triumphs and tragedies, their "chosen" glories and traumas (Volkan, 1991). Sometimes both are contained and condensed into one. In a paper on "Trauma, Memory and Memorials," Michael Rowlands (1998) asks "why some monuments 'work' at the personal level of healing and reconciliation whilst others evoke distaste and condemnation" (1998, p. 54). I add to this the question of how a consultant or applied social scientist can be of help to a community, organization, or culture in helping to foster this reconciliation and healing. It is one thing to observe and interpret how and what groups remember and forget through their memorials. It is another to be asked, invited, to play some role in recommending how, and where, and what, of remembering and memorializing.

Here I am less thinking strictly of design and architecture (which are certainly not the only tangible ways of remembering) as I am thinking of fostering an emotional atmosphere of listening deeply (Stein, 1994a) in which the fullness of grief can wend its way into creative work. My emphasis is on the process: I trust the "outcome" to take care of itself. Psychoanalyst James Masterson (1983), in a context of training, likewise stresses that "You are the servant of a process." To borrow Bion and Winnicott's concepts, I trust the content to take shape so long as it is "contained" in a safe "holding environment" in which anxiety may be expressed and processed. I expect that a memorial cultivated in this way, will foster further mourning, integration, differentiation, and, in turn, resilience, both in its creation and by those who visit it.

Certainly memorials and memorialization can serve aggrandizement and bitterness as "paranoid-schizoid" forms of healing (Klein, 1946). They can also serve to help continue the mourning process as more "depressive" styles of healing (Klein, 1946). The former would become volatile symptoms as well as symbols; they would help incite action that aspires magically to reverse if not undo the fact of the disaster and loss. The latter might lead to action, but of a more secure, serene, kind.

Mourning that is fruition rather than defense allows both a remembering and a forgetting. The forgetting is a gradual letting go, a part of a larger synthesis or reorganization, rather than an all-or-nothing repudiation or repression. The remembering is a sometimes fond, sometimes painful, recollection, rather than a compulsive clinging or stylization. If the process of mourning is full, honest, and possesses integrity—words not usually associated with grief—the memorial and memorialization will be also. "Applied" social science and consulting function best when they can help committees, organizations, communities, and cultures to navigate these turbulent emotional waters.

CONCLUSIONS, IMPLICATIONS, AND RECOMMENDATIONS: WE CAN'T LEARN FROM SOMETHING WE TRY ENTIRELY TO PREPARE FOR

It is emotionally tempting to try to "tie up all loose ends" and tightly "package" recommendations at the end of a chapter, especially when the subject is as destructive as a disaster such as the death of six firefighters on December 3, 1999, in the Worcester Cold Storage and Warehouse fire. Consider the firefighter as a person and as metaphor. Not only is there is a certain social role for people who try to put out literal fires, but there is also the popular notion and image of much corporate and organizational problem solving as "putting out fires all the time." I do not equate them, but I draw attention to the fact that much of everyday cultural workplace life and language have something of the dramatic intensity of "crisis management." Managers and bosses are often known to say: "All I get done around here is going from fire to fire, putting out fires everywhere." The task is of rescuing something or someone from the brink of disaster. The danger is of being consumed by the conflagration oneself—if only by one's own disastrous, devouring anxiety.

Even as we keep the emergency metaphor for part of the story, what can we learn from other parts of it? In this concluding section, I offer some suggestions about what this framework implies. Even in the face of *compelling story-lines or disaster narrative forms*, can we allow ourselves to imagine, even to listen to, alternatives? Catastrophes rarely, if ever, happen neutrally. They happen to people and places that have some significance. The Worcester Cold Storage and Warehouse had been a massive, century-old building near the downtown area, one that most people could identify, and one that firefighters knew in their fears. The building had been insulated in multiple layers of materials, largely petroleum-based. The site, the place, the fire, and the men who "fight" fires were all symbols.

Consider next, notions of healing or simply of helping. An *absolutist*, perhaps official, view designates, "What you should do...," and "Who you should talk to...." What I would call a *naturalist*—not a relativist—view might ask the questions, say, to firefighters or to emergency room staff: "What do you need now?" or "Who do you already talk to…?" These differences pervade the who, what, when, where, how, issues. The point is to not presume what others need or want in times of disaster, but to ask them, to enlist their participation in the mastery of their own circumstances. To return to the firefighting metaphor: Help them to put the out the *figurative* as well as literal fire; do it *with* them. The same applies to timetables for recovery and understandings of how recovery (or substitute other words) happens: ask, don't merely tell. There might not yet be the relationship in which your "telling" is acceptable. "What helps?" is no simple, self-evident question. It is rife with anxiety, with assumptions, and with agendas.

Next, consider the fact that during and following a disaster there are *multiple, often competing frameworks, viewpoints, starting points, feelings, narratives, and agendas*. Stating "whose" event and "what kind of" event it is—let alone becomes—is far from simple. Disaster, like much of culture, is as much the language of argument as it is of consensus. On December 3, 1999, and thereafter, there were many fires in the imagination, not only a single one. The fire in Worcester rapidly spread from a local into a national event. The funeral was attended by many public officials, including the President. The August 2000 issue of *Esquire* featured a lengthy story and pictorial on the fire and on the six firemen who died (Flynn, 2000). It became an American saga—a lucrative one.

Next, the unit(s) of care—who all are affected, and how—cannot be entirely known beforehand or through the imposition of external categories. The same external trauma can have many different "effects" on people. This fact directs us to the inner and outer reaction to the disaster as much as to the disaster itself (La Barre, 1971). This reaction may, in turn, come to be experienced to be part of the disaster. Related to the question of *unit*, are those of *duration, preparedness, the multiplicity rather than the singularity of response, rationality and irrationality of response, style of mourning, and usefulness or effectiveness of help*, among others. We can, paradoxically, plan better for catastrophes if we can accept that (a) irrespective how prepared we are, at least some facets of the next disaster will take us by surprise; (b) resilience is largely a function of the values, attitudes, strengths, and childhood experiences *brought to* the disaster *in interaction with* the availability of a "holding environment" (Winnicott, 1958) to "contain" (Bion, 1956, 1957, 1977) and help process the emotions that emerge, both short-term and long-term, following the disaster. Disaster planning is best that is not manic-inspired.

Containment and *mastery* are vital parts of the mourning and reorganization process precisely because disaster consists of an event of such devastating, overwhelming proportions that could not be contained and mastered at the time. Part of the letting-go of the past in the future, rather than repeating it, is (a) acceptance that the terrible event already occurred and cannot be prevented from happening, and (b) acceptance of one's part, small or large, in the fact that it happened.

The *symbolism of place* and of disaster, that is, the *sense of place* and what takes place in it, influences the direction and outcome of mourning. Attention to the *language* of disaster is part of healing and of helping. In disaster there is not only loss of life and property, but at least a threatened loss of identity—not only *what we have*, but *who we are.* Identity and its politics also affects recovery after disaster.

I conclude with an image. The developmental task of catastrophic loss is the "digestion" and "metabolization" of the event. If the disaster cannot be absorbed and used by the "organism," it will remain swallowed whole, and take on a life as a permanently installed foreign object that will continue to haunt its host (introject). Whatever else we label individual, family, workplace, community, and cultural response to disaster, the ultimate measure of its adaptability lies in how much it helps or interferes with this process of digestion and metabolization—integration. *The distinction between the fullness of mourning and the inability to mourn* (Mitscherlich and Mitscherlich, 1967/1975*) would seem to lie at the heart of the question of how long a fire burns and how long a shadow any disaster casts.* Long after the fire itself is extinguished, its passion continues to burn, and its significance enflames memory. The question of how long this symbolic fire burns is largely a question of the *human space* we create in our communities to hold, contain, and process its still emotionally hot coals. In disasters as in other problem solving, we will do well if we allow our metaphoric cream of wheat to be lumpy and not obligate it to be smooth. In doing so, we are being true to reality and to the people whom we are trying to understand and to help.

In this chapter, a thread throughout the diverse material on the meaning of and adaptation to disaster is the relation between loss and mourning. It is part of the "crust" and "core." The work of mourning—and massive individual and group defenses against it—is a kind of "sub-text" to the process of social change. I shall focus on this largely unconsciously-driven process in the chapter that follows.

Six

Mourning and Society

Situating Loss and Grief in the History and Philosophy of Science

So teach us to number our days,
That we may get us a heart of wisdom.
Psalm 90: 12

INTRODUCTION: MOURNING'S COPERNICAN REVOLUTION

It is psychologically and aesthetically fitting for this book to conclude with a chapter that focuses on the place mourning holds in the life of society. Mourning's presence has been felt in the previous studies in this book. Here it takes center stage in the understanding of unconscious determinants of American—and every society's—culture. Put differently, mourning is often the "core" to culture's "crust."

In its literal sense, the term "Copernican Revolution" refers to a radical reorientation in thinking about the earth's relationship to the sun and other planets. Nicolaus Copernicus (1473-1543), founder of scientific astronomy, proposed that the earth and other planets revolved around the sun, rather than the universe around the earth. Since that time, the phrase has come to be used as a metaphor that signifies a way of thinking that at least has the potential for reconfiguring what we know, how we know, and how we think about ourselves. The notion of *mourning*—its own labyrinthine emotional process, together with the individual, family, workplace, religious, and societal bulwarks against it—constitutes yet another metaphoric Copernican Revolution in the history of ideas and in the application of ideas to help a suffering humanity. The legacy of Sigmund Freud's "Mourning and Melancholia" (1917/1957) in the psychoanalytic study of history and society includes the work of Alexander and Margarete Mitscherlich, Henry Krystal, George Pollock, Vamık Volkan, Martin Wangh, Carl Nedelmann, Maurice Apprey, and Avner Falk, among others.

The reach of mourning—and of its failures—is enormous. No facet of social life is beyond its grasp and influence. It has consequences and leaves footprints in every realm of society. Mourning is a process and theme that links societies and eras throughout human history like Ariadne's Thread. Groups everywhere elaborate specific meanings, symbols, mortuary rites, and other stylizations that deal with individual death. In this chapter I attend to universal issues and conflicts people in every group must face in relation to the reified group itself such as grieving and not grieving loss, metabolizing and repeating loss, and working through and "freezing" loss. What happens when the group loses, or feels in danger of losing, not a "member," but "itself," phenomenologically experienced as a symbolic object? For example, the destruction of the Holy Temple, Jerusalem being laid in ruins, and people being cast into exile was and is experienced both literally, by Jews, and as a human metaphor. What happens when the membrane of meaning and of living "our way" is threatened, punctured, and penetrated, and it disintegrates? Since any notion of "social skin" is ultimately metaphoric, how shall we understand it and our responses to its loss?

Approached in this way, mourning has importance for the history of ideas, not only for specialists in fields such as psychoanalysis and anthropology. At the same time, attention to conscious and unconscious mental life is essential for the explication of the process of mourning over history and society. In both cases, communication between mental-health professionals, historians, anthropologists, and diplomats is essential for understanding and aiding societies.

The vicissitudes of any group identity—from national to professional, from religious to corporate—are bound up with experiences of loss and adaptation to it. The same holds true for geopolitical arrangements and their psycho-histories. Human group boundaries, together with their ideologies, are heirs to issues of loss, separation, anxiety, and grief. It is always presumptuous (as it is tempting) to claim to have discovered *the* Rosetta Stone in any field of inquiry, let alone between fields of inquiry. The concept of "mourning" does not magically make all history and society decipherable, but it renders much comprehensible that has been shrouded in mystery and mystification. Perhaps a better metaphor is Ariadne's Thread in the labyrinth ruled by the Minotaur of ignorance.

My goal in this chapter will be less to situate the "group" elaboration of mourning within specifically psychoanalytic and anthropological (or other disciplinary) schemes, as it will be to locate "mourning" in relation to group or society as a fundamentally revolutionary way of thinking about culture, history, politics, and social process in general. Much as I draw from psychoanalytic and anthropological thought, the scope of mourning is too vast to limit its discussion to specific fields of inquiry such as psychoanalysis or the social sciences. At the same time, the influence of the unconscious deserves to be central to understanding all aspects of thinking about social process. This is why I have subtitled this chapter: "An Essay in the History and Philosophy of Science."

Let me briefly situate myself in relation to the subject. Having studied Euro-American ethnicity and nationalism earlier in my career, I have more recently come to study what is euphemistically called massive "managed social change" in workplace organizations. These go by such names as downsizing, rightsizing, RIFing, reduction in force, reengineering, restructuring, outsourcing, deskilling, surplusing, and corporate-managed healthcare (Stein, 1998a, 1998b, 2000, 2001c; see also Hughes, 2000; Precker, 2001). These studies come out of day-to-day work as a clinical teacher in a health-sciences center, as an organizational consultant, and as a participant and presenter at national conferences in many disciplines. I have also learned more than I bargained for from the 1995 Oklahoma City bombing, the 1999 central Oklahoma tornadoes, the 1999 Columbine High School shooting, and the 1999 fire in Worcester, Massachusetts.

I have come to identify the triad of change-loss-grief as a fundamental unit of experience at the group as well as the individual level. Furthermore, I see much continuity in unconscious and conscious process between many types of distinct social units and experiences (e.g., ethnic, national, religious, organizational workplace, migration, terrorism, and war) in the group psychology of response to catastrophic change.

MOURNING: SOME THEORETICAL CONSIDERATIONS

To begin with, mourning is a facet of our human biology. At its best, its ideal, it is a renewing process, adaptive to separation and loss. For us, the human primate, all change involves loss. All loss unleashes mourning and defenses against mourning both in the individual and in others. Both what is lost and the process of mourning are rife with symbolism.

One not only loses ambivalently loved whole persons. One also loses more primitively loved parts and pieces of persons, representations of persons, and the psychological functions of persons. Further, one loses symbols of people and of relationships with people: territories, wars, homelands, jobs, homes, and political campaigns. Just as loss and mourning are heirs to what psychoanalysts call "drives" and "drive derivatives," so are they also heirs to what one might call often-shared *symbolically-charged object derivatives*. When we lose someone, we also lose something else—emotionally charged "function(s)."

What Volkan calls (1981) "linking phenomena" and "linking objects" in individually short-circuited mourning, has as its group psychodynamic counterparts *social linking phenomena and social linking objects* in tribes, ethnic groups, and nations. Through these symbols, the dead are revived, kept alive, killed off, and revived again. Here, the complicated, bizarre work of mourning takes place entirely outside the self; it feels like the opposite of inner grieving. Still, even "uncomplicated" mourning is quite complicated. One only wishes that it were a simple, direct, independent variable! Sometimes it feels like a hopelessly dependent variable, instead (on the crucial role of shame, see Gruen, 1999).

Mourning confronts us with the paradox of vulnerability. If mourning is a natural response to loss, it is also among the most vulnerable of human conditions. When we grieve, we yield to feelings, fantasies, and memories. We do not protect and hold back. In mourning, we lower the shield. Vulnerability is essential to allow the process to continue and to be able to work through the mourning. That vulnerability is mourning's—and our—strength. Containment and processing in a loving holding environment (to borrow from W. R. Bion and D. W. Winnicott) are what allows the internal work of mourning to proceed. We need to create culturally safe spaces for its processing. Yet we rarely do. Even the inwardness of mourning is profoundly intersubjective.

Despite its ritualization in various tribal, ethnic, and national groups, we humans often regard mourning as unbearable weakness and burden. Through groups—society—we gird ourselves with defenses that promise invulnerability and invincibility. We structure into our lives enemies, allies, terrors, and terrorists (Volkan, 1988, 1997) as means of protecting ourselves from the vulnerabilities of bereavement. Yet these defenses set up cycles of future endangerment greater than any regression in the service of mourning.

For instance, the inter-generational transmission of (failed) mourning (Volkan, 1997) obligates future generations to repeat and relive the traumatic horrors of parental and ever-more-remote generations. What is less often said is that to a large degree, much of what we think of as "cultural continuity" among ethnic, religious, and national groups rests upon an inter-generational, ritually dramatized, transmission institutionalized in rituals, symbols, values, and meanings. A large part of the work of culture "itself" is an embodiment and enactment of "the inability to mourn" (Mitscherlich & Mischerlich, 1967/1975). Mourning is necessary to transcendence. Its absence assures fixity and repetition and ever-renewed historical trauma. The recognition of the breadth of group loss and mourning in the wake of recent school and workplace shootings in the United States has led to the training and deployment of cadres of "grief counselors" to disaster sites.

This perspective commends certain questions, or at least viewpoints, for understanding all group-trauma and their aftermath: *What was lost? And: What is being mourned (or cannot, must not, be mourned)?* As we develop more inclusive theories and more psychodynamically informed taxonomies of trauma, loss, and grief, we must offer greatest fidelity to experience. It will teach us what we need to know and correct what we think we already know (see Du Plessix Gray, 2000).

LOCATING MOURNING IN ORDINARY GROUP LIFE

The work of Track Two Diplomacy (unofficial diplomacy) and the study of social loss, social meaning, and its vicissitudes by the Center for the Study of Mind and Human Interaction (CSMHI) and others has involved discovering, exhuming, and systematically studying a subject the process of which is at the core of human development and all experience: namely, mourning. And despite our coercive cultural doctrine of solitary mourning ("Have a good cry; get over it; and get a life."), Freud and Bion have reminded us that all human psychology is ultimately group psychology. The Kleinian dyad of mother and infant is as much an intersubjective human biology as it is human psychology; and it in turn is embedded in the family-group. I allow myself several "random" examples to illustrate the generality of group mourning in the life of human groups.

Thirty-five or so years ago, I avidly read accounts of the crisis in physics during the end of the nineteenth century and the beginning of the twentieth century. Among the writers were Ernest Rutherford, Max Planck, Niels Bohr, Max Born, Erwin Schrödinger, Werner Heisenberg, and Albert Einstein. I remember reading about sleeplessness and about solitary walks in the woods to make sense of a world at increasing conflict with new data from that world. From the sense of chaos and torment in these retrospective histories by the pioneers of relativity and quantum physics, I could sense that something more was at stake than strictly mathematics and physics alone. I can now identify through words and clear feelings the experiences they were describing. More than strictly intellectual excitement, there was a sense of anxiety, dread, and loss. There was as much an experience of a crisis of identity (Erik Erikson's concept) in this displacement in time and space, as there was in any immigrant individual or wave. There was a sense of the ending of a world, in history as well as in space; destruction and loss were part of the new creation.

The worldview bequeathed by Newton and Galileo, one that had held the world together for nearly three centuries, was now collapsing and disintegrating before disconfirming evidence. The scientific wisdom of the past no longer sufficed, and any new coherence was still in the future. Whatever else these great scientists and thinkers were doing, they were also doing the work of mourning. They did not have the classic schizophrenic's world-destruction fantasy. They were at once the heirs of that destruction and active architects of it. Deep grief was part of the eventual scientific renewal. In short, what I could not realize thirty-five years ago was that "even" a major social revolution in the history of scientific ideas had to pass through the flames and tears of mourning.

I expect that we are more familiar, and emotionally comfortable, with thinking of catastrophic social change, loss, and grief as associated with the "crisis cults" and "ghost dances" of primitive and historical peoples and the vicissitudes of their world views (La Barre, 1971, 1972). It gives us the satisfaction of at least some cultural and temporal distance from ourselves. Yet, science and scientists—and their societies—meld theory and method into identity and become as confounded as any tribalist when the destruction of worlds portends. The revulsion with which Nazis greeted Einstein's relativity—*Abscheulich*, repulsive, they named it—was the same sentiment that greeted the revolutionary music of Beethoven, Wagner, and Stravinsky. Worlds that could not be grieved and then opened, were instead slammed shut from within like a vault.

Historians and philosophers of Western science are fond of enumerating the many severe "hammer blows" scientific theories and theorists have inflicted upon our claim to a special place in the universe. Copernicus, Kepler, and Galileo removed the earth from the center of the universe. Darwin took the human primate out of the realm of angels and planted us firmly into mammalian biology and natural history. Einstein (and his colleagues and successors in relativity and quantum physics) introduced perspective or viewpoint as part of any statement of truth. Freud found that *Homo sapiens* was a far less reasoning and reasonable creature than we had thought. Less familiar assaults are the discoveries of W. R. Bion on the irrationality that percolates through the decision-making and tasks of ostensibly reality-oriented work-groups. One could continue almost indefinitely to enumerate additional "narcissistic blows" science has dealt to Western human certainty.

Yet most analyses miss the crucial point that, individually and cumulatively, these scientific revolutions provoked an overwhelming sense of loss, disorientation, and mourning—and attempts to reverse the loss. (Did not even the mythic Narcissus turn "narcissistic" only upon the loss of his beloved Echo?) Our cultural landscape is strewn and littered with hosts of "linking objects" through which the faithful strive to keep the old faith—and its symbolic fathers and mothers—alive. The crisis of faith in one's worldview—projectively and introjectively experienced as the world itself—led to numerous "crisis cults" (Devereux, 1955; La Barre, 1971, 1972) that rested at least in part on the defensive inability to mourn. Many of today's ideological fundamentalisms draw their narcissistic energy and collective support in part from the retreat from the mourning that would be required to relinquish the Old World.

For instance, the Counter-Reformation in Christendom drew much of its strength from the loss and threat posed by the Reformation. Galileo escaped execution at the hands of the Inquisition by publicly recanting his radical cosmology—one which threatened the Ptolemaic earth-centered cosmology upon which the Church had relied. The new cosmology, in turn, threatened this astronomical "rock." If I may shift cultural realms and eras, one could make similar formulations about change, loss, and short-circuited mourning in the history of musical ideas: for instance in the cases of Beethoven, Wagner, Mahler, Stravinsky, and Shostakovich.

Let me now leap ahead to the beginning of the twenty-first century. Daniel Barenboim scheduled the performance of the first act of *Die Walküre*, by Richard Wagner, at the Israel Festival on July 7, 2001 (Chism, 2001). It was the third or fourth time in the past twenty years that he and conductor Zubin Mehta had attempted to have any music by Wagner performed in Israel. The previous times, the widespread angry protests shouted down any hearing of the music of a composer who had been adopted as a hero by the Third Reich. At the July 2001 festival, protesters were asked by other audience members to leave after a half-hour debate over the performance of music by Hitler's favorite composer. Those who disagreed walked out of the theater, some shouting insults as they left. Wagner represents the still-keen sense of outrage and still-raw grief among many Israelis toward the Nazi era and its dedication to eliminating every Jew from the face of the earth.

Wagner—as-representation of trauma, loss, and grief—is a superb "test," as it were, of the relative power of event *in relation to* the relative power of symbol, for many Jews in foreign ("diaspora") lands are avid concert-goers to the music of Wagner. Indeed, since the earliest days of Wagner's music, many Jewish conductors have numbered among his finest interpreters. The path of social mourning is never simple.

The early twenty-first century has also witnessed the completion of the mapping of the human genome and the announcement of the prospect of cloning humans. Among the first uses for which it is projected is to reverse profound loss. The February 19, 2001, cover of *Time* pictured the large faces of two babies mirroring one another, their tiny noses almost meeting in the middle of the page. Its exact bilateral symmetry reminded me of a Rorschach inkblot. In the gap between their eyes and foreheads, the caption read: "Human Cloning Is Closer Than You Think." Beneath the chin of the baby to the left reads: "For couples who can't have a child—or who have lost one—the unthinkable may soon be possible. Here are the perils." On the two-page spread that begins the article (in the "Society" section), identical babies are pictured as coming down a conveyor belt, as in a manufacturing plant. To return to the cover image, one component of the fantasy seems to be the split between death and life, dead baby and live baby. Through science we hope to realize—that is, to make real—the fantasy of magically reversed death. In effect, we turn the cloned baby into a "linking object," condemning him or her to live on the edge of life and death. The cloned baby is destined to be haunted by the dead child it replaces. Life becomes death's double. Upon a single canvas, the couple's grief and society's fantasy converge, implemented by the priesthood of medical science.

Early in the narrative, Nancy Gibbs (2001) writes: "Imagine for a moment that your daughter needs a bone-marrow transplant and no one can provide a match, that your wife's early menopause has made her infertile; or that your five year-old has drowned in a lake and that your grief has made it impossible to get your mind around the fact that he is gone forever.... [Questions immediately arise:] Our two-year-old daughter died in a car crash; we saved a lock of her hair in a baby book. Can you clone her? ..." (p. 47). We flaunt fantasies of omnipotent fertility, realized by medical technology, in the face of death. A magical reversal of time seemingly makes mourning unnecessary. It is as if to say, "Why grieve when you can clone?" What quickly turns into a biomedical ethics issue is, at root, an enactment of the inability to mourn.

In a thoughtful editorial, columnist Ellen Goodman (2001) describes a group of scientists named Clonaid, who offer soon to store cells from a beloved person in order to create a clone if the person dies. She comments: "They justify and sell cloning with the promise that you needn't mourn a child. You can resurrect him....The phony, manipulative attempt to justify reproduction as resurrection makes even the dangers of duplication pale in comparison." Goodman concludes, "there is something... unethical about those hucksters of hope who sell cloning as an antidote to mourning. It is nothing but a dose of denial" (p. 15A).

Via genetic engineering, the society-wide idealization of technological solutions serves as a cultural defense against intimacy, loss, and grief (Stein & Hill, 1988). Both literally and figuratively, cloning may come to be the focus of a twenty-first century counterpart to preliterate societies "crisis cults." In short, the idea and process of mourning would seem to permeate—if not generate—a host of social processes and issues, historic and contemporary.

THE CAUSE(S) OF WORLD WAR II AND THEORIES OF MOURNING

I turn now to a subject that has occupied some of the best minds in the past sixty years. The long-standing debate over the origins and causes of World War II illustrates, among other things, the complexity and subtleties of mourning. To my thinking, it also situates the issue of mourning centrally in the history of ideas—and the ideas of history. One of the major lessons in the study of social mourning is that things are rarely what they seem. The path to understanding and explanation is serpentine. To use a different metaphor, cultural symbols, like dreams, are the work of condensation. Furthermore, practitioners and scholars become highly invested in their theories and models.

Consider now World War II, for example. One can look virtually anywhere and recognize the presence of mourning—along with its disguises and diversions. The Soviets, and now the Russians, have long mythologized and ritualized the horrors of "The Great Patriotic War," as they have called it, and focus on the slaughter of their people and devastation of their landscape by the Nazi Germans. Even terrible reality, though, can be brought into the orbit of fantasy and defense. Specifically, the enormous suffering and internal slaughter of the Russian (and Soviet, and other Slavic) people(s) under their own leader Josef Stalin, from the mid-1930s until his death in 1952, has been given far less attention. Chiefly via displacement and projection, mourning of the losses in World War II bears the burden of the "impacted mourning" (Shatan, 1997) from the brutalized and terrorized life in the Stalin era—much of which was endured prior to World War II. For a time, the search for and the war against an external enemy could contain and divert both the (largely unconscious) rage and grief over the Stalinist war against his own peoples.

At the more abstract and general level, what can be said is inseparable from what cannot; what may be felt is inseparable from what may not; what is remembered (and grieved) is inseparable from what must be forgotten; and what may be mourned is inseparable from what may not be mourned. Culture, history, memory, and mourning are entwined in a unitary process.

Let me broaden the issue of mourning and causality in relation to World War II. One theory holds that the trauma of World War I (or, alternately, the punitive Treaty of Versailles) was unmournable and thereby set the stage for revenge via the Second World War. Here, the Second World War is an attempt to restage the prior trauma and reverse the humiliation (Binion, 1975, 1981, 2003). Binion writes of the psychological fit of leader and led after trauma: "Historically, traumatized groups often do their reliving [of trauma] through leaders who relive traumas of their own in the process" (2003, p. 2). A second theory holds that brutal German childhood and child-rearing, represented in German mythology and folklore, could not be mourned and worked though and thus set the stage for collective repetition through action in World War II (Miller, 1983). A third theory focuses on widespread father-absence in post-World War I Germany due to their deaths on the battlefield, the consequence of their absence for gender identity, and the resolution of oedipality among the cohort of children and youth (Loewenberg, 1971). Still a fourth theory holds that in massive trauma of any type, the characteristic response is that of post-traumatic stress disorder (PTSD) and not that of grief and mourning over loss (Mitchell & Everly, 1995). This model, popular among the American "school" of Critical Incident Stress Management (and Debriefing), radically distinguishes trauma from loss-induced grief, both in explanation and in assumptions about how best to respond to suffering. One wonders how, and whether, these models—all of which draw upon the dynamics of mourning, but the mourning of widely differing "objects"—can be reconciled, even integrated (See Kren & Rappoport, 1980/1994; Rando, 1994, 1996).

In addition to being a cultural and historical event, World War II offers a kind of "test case" for the understanding of the complexity and subtlety of group mourning. I suggest that just as the processes of serving as container, holding environment, and processor of unconscious material are essential to group mourning on the historical and clinical stages, they are also essential capabilities in the work of a scholar who encounters competing theories, and emotionally overwhelming mourning, in relation to the "material" being studied. An attitude of "not knowing," of hovering curiosity akin to Freud's notion of "evenly-suspended attention" (1912/1958, pp. 111-112), helps one to avoid premature and defensive closure in understanding World War II and other massive group trauma.

THE END OF THE COLD WAR AND THE INABILITY TO MOURN

I have argued thus far that the *idea* of mourning and of defenses against it help to account for a wide array of otherwise mystifying phenomena. My final consideration in this chapter will be the worldwide eruption of ethnic, national, and religious war, of terrorism, and of domestic violence in the United States since the early 1990s. In the middle 1990s, during a conversation I remember blurting out that "We all live in Bosnia now." I was metaphorically referring to the "ethnic cleansing" taking place by Bosnian Serbs against Bosnian Muslims and to the wider bloodshed between Bosnian Serbs, Croats, and

Muslims. Brutality and terror had erupted in the United States as well. Names such as Bosnia, Gaza, West Bank (Jordan), Iraq, Rwanda, Chechnya, Somalia, Kenya, Kosovo, and Timor, and numerous school and workplace shootings and bombings in the United States immediately come to mind. [This chapter was written before the September 11, 2001, attacks on New York City and Washington, D.C. These events now join the list.]

Particularistic studies have contributed much to understanding these conflicts. But strictly local studies lack a key, and ubiquitous, ingredient, one with massive change and loss at its core. I refer to the collapse of communism in the Soviet Union, the breakup of the Soviet Empire, and the end of the Cold War in 1990. The persecutory terror of the opposition between the Soviet and American empires had unconsciously stabilized the world since the end of the Second World War. Worldwide euphoria quickly dissolved into worldwide conflict.

If, to Americans, the "Evil Empire" was gone, then from the viewpoint of the world (including Americans), the geopolitical opposition that had sustained the emotional structure of much of the world for decades had disappeared. The end of the prospect of nuclear winter did not give way to a lasting spring. The 1991 Gulf War—principally between the U.S. and Iraq—almost immediately ensued. President George Bush claimed to preside over a "New World Order" as the old order was collapsing. Insurrections and boundary violations erupted everywhere.

The loss of the terrible emotional security provided by the opposition of East and West was not mourned, could not be mourned. It gave way to the free-floating anxiety and the search for new enemies upon which to focus one's aggression and thereby attempt to reconsolidate a group sense of self (group identity). Little effort was devoted by the group members or by their leaders to grieving the loss or to accepting as one's own the parts of oneself released by the loss. Instead, most effort was directed toward opening old group wounds and grievances and toward realizing them in vendettas ranging from terrorism to war.

To borrow from Volkan's work on "linking objects and linking phenomena" (1981), and to apply them to the group-level, one might say that with the end of the Cold War there erupted emotionally the frantic search for new *group linking objects*, specifically, new enemy-groups in which the dead, real and symbolic, could be revived and killed again and again. With the fall of a bipolar world based on empires, and of a "third world" between them, the experience of loss and regression led to a search to reorganize around what I have called a "good enough enemy." Ideologies based on ethnicity, nationalism, and religion quickly filled the emotional gap left by the political bankruptcy of previously unifying ideologies based on social class and economics.

To conclude this section, I would like to describe two images that bring these abstract ideas "home." The first is a cartoon that appeared in the April 7, 2001, issue of *The Dallas Morning News*, p. 31A. Its message is mourning and defenses against it. The cartoon is by Mike Peters/*Dayton Daily News*. The cartoon is in two frames, which read left to right. In the left frame, a big-eared President Bush is saying: "My administration has a plan to end global warming...." The second frame, to the right, pictures President Bush standing halfway inside a bomb shelter, about to close the hatch at the top. He is saying: "We're bringing back the Cold War." Even more explicitly, the April 23, 2001, cover of *The New Republic* depicts mainland Chinese soldiers, bearing machine guns, marching in military parade toward the camera (reader). At the front of the line, a soldier carries a bright red flag. In the lower middle of the page, the caption in bold black letters reads: "An Enemy for Our Time." Even after eleven years, there are strong echoes of the end of the Cold War and of the incomplete mourning of its occurrence.

CONCLUSIONS: TRANSCENDING SOCIAL TRAUMA AND REPETITION

In this chapter, I have considered mourning to be a central concept in the history and philosophy of science. I have considered mourning from the viewpoint of the *human group (and its symbols) as the object of separation and loss and mourning*, rather than only from the viewpoint of the individual who dies and is mourned. I have offered an admittedly patchwork series of examples to illustrate the range of subjects group mourning of "itself" encompasses.

I have suggested that this kind of mourning cuts across countless social units, eras, and processes—religion, science, nationalism, diplomacy, workplace organizations, medicine, the arts—and deserves to be thought of as a central organizing concept in the history of mankind. I have also suggested that if mourning is a "natural" response to loss, defense against mourning is equally "natural." Massive social protection arrangements—amounting to protection rackets—wall off even deeper, more personal vulnerabilities. If our species "succeeds" in destroying itself, it may be due more to the complications of mourning than to the unleashing of pure aggressive drive. Aggression, in service of preserving the unmournable self (and its group aspect, the unmournable "pseudospecies"), may immolate the planet.

In this brief concluding section, I consider whether transcendence of the often manic flight from mourning—even in the midst of official and formal mourning rituals!—is possible, and the shape such transcendence might take. Forgiveness *of* history and forgiveness *in* history would seem to be the fundamental processes in the "change of heart" that liberates people from repetition, allows the introduction of something genuinely new, and leads to resilience—even if only for a time. The Marshall Plan following World II is a "collective" example. There are many "personal" examples, even in recent memory: such leaders as Mahatma Gandhi, Martin Luther King, Jr., Anwar Sadat, Mikhail Gorbachev, Bishop Desmond Tutu, and Nelson Mandela are among the most outstanding. Sadly, unconsciously driven social forces may overtake and reverse changes in course begun by reparative leaders. Still, we are beginning to understand the dynamics and the kind of change necessary to nurture the difficult working-through in mourning.

What, in one perspective, is "clinical" medicine carried out in the small group, becomes, in another perspective, "preventive" medicine carried out in the community and international settings (Volkan, 2000). Volkan and his colleagues have shown, I believe, that through mourning, one (and one's group) may pursue social justice without inflicting vengeful injustice in the process. For, through mourning, the "other" comes to be experienced as a truly distinct, separate human being and group, and is not experienced as only the projective embodiment of a disavowed part of the self.

Rafael Moses (1990), for instance, discusses acknowledgment as the balm of narcissistic injuries. In order to be able to acknowledge another person and group, one must first lower and grieve one's shield of grandiosity—and rediscover the circumstances under which it was fashioned and raised. Such acknowledgment would seem to be at the root of much disaster prevention and the facilitation of mourning.

Conventionally, the "great leaps forward" in the West have been seen in realms of industrialization, economic globalization, and in the technological unification of the world via the Internet. An even more urgent leap, though, is no single surmounting of a hurdle, but a process of countless small steps: the mourning of the perfection and of the immortality of those various groups of which we call ourselves "members." The future of an illusion applies to our inseparability from human groups as much as it applies to the objects of our religious devotion. To the condensation (not merely a list) of all that we have lost, and of all that we are mourning, we must now add our groups "themselves" as ambivalently beloved symbolic objects.

I conclude with a personal anecdote. In September 1995, six months after the bombing of the federal building in Oklahoma City, I gave a talk at the Center for the Study of Mind and Human Interaction on disaster and mourning. During that talk, I handed a piece of granite from the bombed building around the room. Five months earlier, shortly after the late-May implosion of the federal building, a nurse had offered me a piece of granite from the Murrah Building in gratitude for my own small contribution of counseling and consulting behind-the-official-scenes. At first I treasured it. I kept it close by in my office. I brought it to many talks I gave on the bombing. Now, several years later, I have discovered that I have misplaced, perhaps permanently lost, the sacred rock. At first, I searched frantically for it, feeling guilty, ashamed of losing it. Of all people, I should have been able to keep track of it. As time went on, I came to see and to accept the loss of the rock as part of my own grief and trauma resolution. In a way, my tangible memorial gradually dissolved into space and time. Unconsciously, I allowed it to. As I attempt to understand, and to help others in, subsequent catastrophes, I find myself less obsessively cluttered by this past.

As a species, we have already put men on the moon. The distance to the moon, though, is shorter than to the human heart. It is the inner and intersubjective spaces that are more distant and daunting. Nowhere is this truer than in loss and mourning.

Epilogue

The purpose of an epilogue should be to close one door in the hope that others will have been opened. In bringing this book to a close, I briefly reaffirm the method that underlies the diversity of cultural materials presented.

In this book I have offered six "case" studies in the contemporary United States as examples of the usefulness of a psychodynamic approach to understanding culture—any culture. They have covered such topics as the September 11, 2001, attacks on New York City and Washington, D.C., the April 20, 1999, shootings at Columbine High School, the execution of Timothy McVeigh, the many faces of hypernationalism and xenophobia, the December 3, 1999, fire in Worcester, Massachusetts, and other disasters, and the relationship between mourning and society.

The method of each chapter has been to begin with conventional, often culturally stylized understandings and explanations, and, by attending closely to other cultural materials at hand, to arrive at broader and deeper psychodynamically informed understandings and explanations. This is the essence of the utility of psychoanalysis as applied to groups rather than exclusively to individuals in clinical situations such as psychotherapy.

The approach taken in this book suggests that psychodynamic processes are often the underpinnings (the "core") of what we observe on the surface as the "whole" culture (the "crust"). We humans are motivated to want culture to explain itself, for there to be no further accounting. In this respect, post-modernist thought is only a recent variant on groupish narcissism. Yet, if the American studies in this book are even approximately accurate, culture can be understood to rest to a considerable degree upon unconscious, largely irrational, sources. The findings arrived at by this method of inquiry have been corroborated for other cultures and other times by such scholars as George Devereux, Weston La Barre, Melford Spiro, Vamik Volkan, and Richard Koenigsberg.

In studying American culture, I must conclude that our culture less responds to reality as projects conflictual parts of the self onto (into) reality, and from these projections—in concert with other defenses—fashions both culture and reality in the image of the unconscious and defenses against it. Simply put, Americans tend to look for the exclusive source of culture in material, economic reality. By contrast, I have situated much of this presumably palpable reality within cultural values, beliefs, roles, and conflicts, and in turn, within the unconscious forces that give rise to them.

This book has implications for public and national policy as well as for scholarly discourse. We cannot hope to solve clinical, professional, national, and international problems if we do not identify them correctly in the first place. A recognition that we are *unconsciously motivated to solve the wrong problem* is a first step at correcting ourselves. Recognition of the reach of the unconscious in the life of culture holds the promise of liberating us from the cultural prisons in which we confine ourselves. By having greater access to the "core" that is part of the "crust," we are less blindly driven by that "core." We are more whole. This book is a small step in that direction.

About the Author

Howard F. Stein, Ph.D., a psychoanalytic anthropologist, is professor and special assistant to the chair in the Department of Family and Preventive Medicine, University of Oklahoma Health Sciences Center, Oklahoma City, Oklahoma, U.S.A., where he has taught for twenty-five years. He is author, editor, or co-editor of twenty-two books and author of over two hundred scholarly and clinical articles. He edited *The Journal of Psychoanalytic Anthropology* from 1980 to 1988. His most recent book is *Nothing Personal, Just Business: A Guided Journey into Organizational Darkness*, published in 2001. He is past president of the High Plains Society for Applied Anthropology and is currently a member of the committee on the teaching of behavioral sciences in medical education, of the Institute of Medicine of the National Academies, U.S.A.

References

Ablon, J. (1973). Reactions of Samoan burn patients and families to severe burns. *Social Science and Medicine, 7*(3), 167-78.

Allcorn, S. (1994). *Anger in the workplace*. Westport, CT: Quorum.

Allcorn, S. (1998). Foreword. In H. F. Stein, *Euphemism, spin, and the crisis in organizational life.* pp.ix-xiv. Westport, CT: Quorum Books.

Allcorn, S., Baum, H., Diamond, M. A., & Stein, H. F. (1996). *The HUMAN cost of a management failure: Organizational downsizing at General Hospital.* Westport, CT: Quorum Books.

Apprey, M. (1993). Introduction. In M. Apprey & H. F. Stein (Eds.) *Intersubjectivity, projective identification and otherness.* (pp. 1-3). Pittsburgh: Duquesne University Press.

Apprey, M. (2000). *The dazzle of the genital chamber is but an ambush toward death: The analysis of a poet's writing inhibition.* Unpublished book manuscript.

Auden, W. H. (1965). September 1, 1939. In H.P. Simonson (Ed.), *TRIO: A book of stories, plays, and poems* (pp. 624-626). New York: Harper & Row.

Bachelard, G. (1964). *The pychoanalysis of fire.* Boston: Beacon Press.

Barber, B. R. (1996). *Jihad vs. McWorld: How globalism and tribalism are reshaping the world.* New York: Ballantine.

Bartlett, J. (1955). *Familiar quotations.* Boston: Little, Brown and Company.

Batteau, A. W. (2001). Aggressive technology in a century of industrial disasters. *Practicing Anthropology, 23*(4), 28-32.

Beisel, D. R. (1999). Columbine: The search for causes. In P.H. Elovitz (ed.), *The Best of Clio's Psyche, 1994-1999.* (pp. 57-60) Franklin Lakes, NJ: The Psychohistory Forum.

Bennis, W. (1989). *Why leaders can't lead.* San Francisco: Jossey-Bass.

Bernard, K. (1987). *The Maldive chronicles.* New York: Performing Arts Journal Publications.

Binion, R. (1975). *Hitler among the Germans.* New York: Elsevier.

Binion, R. (1981). *Soundings: Psychohistorical and psycholiterary.* New York: Psychohistory Press.

Binion, R. (2003). Bush's America goes to war. *Clio's Psyche, 10*(1): 1-3.

Bion, W. R. (1956). Development of schizophrenic thought. *International Journal of Psycho-Analysis, 37*: 344-346.

Bion, W. R. (1957). The Differentiation of the psychotic from the non-psychotic personalities. *International Journal of Psycho-Analysis, 38*: 266-275.

Bion, W. R. (1962). *Learning from experience.* New York: Basic Books.

Bion, W. R. (1977). *Seven servants.* New York: Jason Aronson.

Blazak, R. (1999). Interview: Youth and hate. *Intelligence Report: The Southern Poverty Law Center, 96*, 24-27.

Blos, P. (1962). *On adolescence: A psychoanalytic interpretation.* New York: Free Press.

Bollas, C. (1989). *In the shadow of the object: Psychoanalysis of the unthought known.* New York: Columbia University Press..

Bousquet, T. (1999, May 11). Disorderly conduct. *Chico Examiner.* Retrieved August 9, 1999, from http://www .chicoexaminer.com

Boyer, L. B. (1999). *Countertransference and regression.* Northvale, NJ: Jason Aronson.

Brody, H. (1987). *Stories of sickness*. New Haven: Yale University Press.

Bursztajn, H. J. (1999, August 4). When health care goes lacking. [Letter to the editor], *The New York Times*, p. A18.

Chism, O. (2001, May 6). Developments of Wagnerian proportions. *The Dallas Morning News*, p. 3C.

Cohen, S. (2001, May 5). America's home grown terrorist. Retrieved June 14, 2001, from (multihome.www.opus1com/ian/PRIVATE/2001/05/05/200105051938 0274.html). .

Couple get probation in fatal fire. (2002, May 31). *The Dallas Morning News*, 12A.

de Mause, L. (1982). *Foundations of psychohistory*. New York: Creative Roots.

de Mause, L. (1984). *Reagan's America*. New York: Creative Roots.

Devereux, G. (1955). Charismatic leadership and crisis. In G. Róheim (Ed.). *Psychoanalysis and the social sciences*, *4*, 145-157. New York: International Universities Press.

Devereux, G. (1956). T*herapeutic education: Its theoretical bases and practice*. New York: Harper.

Devereux, G. (1967). *From anxiety to method in the behavioral sciences*. The Hague: Mouton.

Devereux, G. (1969). Normal and abnormal: The key problem of psychiatric anthropology, In W. Muensterberger (Ed.), *Man and his culture: Psychoanalytic anthropology after Totem and Taboo*. (Pp. 113-136). New York: Taplinger. (Original work published 1956)

Devereux, G. (1980). *Basic problems of ethnopsychiatry*. Chicago: University of Chicago Press.

Devereux, G. & Loeb, E. M. (1943). Antagonistic acculturation. *American Sociological Review*, *7*, 133-147.

De Vos, G. A. (1966). Toward a cross-cultural psychology of caste behavior. In G. A. De Vos & H. Wagatsuma, (Eds.), *Japan's invisible race* (pp. 353-384). Berkeley: University of California Press.

Diamond, M. (1997). Administrative assault: A contemporary psychoanalytic view of violence and aggression in the workplace. *American Review of Public Administration*, *27*(3), 228-247.

Diamond, M. A. (1998). The symbiotic lure: Organizations as defective containers. *Administrative Theory and Praxis*, *20*(3), 315-325.

Doka, K. J. (1989). *Disenfranchised grief*. Lanham, MD: Lexington Books.

Douglas, M. (1992). *Risk and blame: Essays in cultural theory*. London: Routledge.

Douglas, M. & Wildavsky, A. (1982). *Risk and culture: An essay on the selection of technological and environmental dangers*. Berkeley: University of California Press.

Du Plessix Gray, F. (2000). The work of mourning. *The American Scholar*, *69*(3), 7-13.

Dundes, A. (1984). *Life is like a chicken coup ladder: A portrait of German culture through folklore*. New York: Columbia University Press.

Eisenbruch, M. (1984a). Cross-cultural aspects of bereavement. I: A conceptual framework for comparative analysis. *Culture, Medicine and Psychiatry*, *8*(3), 283-309.

Eisenbruch, M. (1984b). Cross-cultural aspects of bereavement. II: Ethnic and cultural variations in the development of bereavement practices. *Culture, Medicine and Psychiatry*, *8*(4), 315-347.

Eisenbruch, M. (1991). From post-traumatic stress to cultural bereavement: diagnosis of Southeast Asian refugees. *Social Science and Medicine, 33*(6), 73-80.

Eisenbruch, M. (1992). Toward a culturally sensitive DSM: Cultural bereavement in Cambodian refugees and the traditional healer as taxonomist. *Journal of Nervous and Mental Diseases, 180*(1), January, 8-10.

Erikson, E. H. (1958). *Young man Luther.* New York: Norton.

Erikson, E. H. (1959). *Identity and the life cycle: Selected essays.* New York: International Universities Press, [*Psychological Issues 1*(1) Monograph].

Erikson, E. H. (1963). *Childhood and society.* Rev. ed. New York: Norton.

Erikson, E.H. (1964). *Insight and responsibility: Lectures on the ethical implications of psychoanalytic insight.* New York: Norton.

Erikson, E. H. (1968). *Identity: Youth and crisis.* New York: Norton

Erikson, K. T. (1976). *Everything in its path: Destruction of community in the Buffalo Creek flood.* New York: Simon and Schuster.

Fallers, L. A. (1974). *The social anthropology of the nation state.* Chicago: Aldine.

Faludi, S. (1999). *Stiffed: The betrayal of the American man.* New York: William Morrow.

Feld, S. & Basso, K. H. (Eds.). (1996). *Senses of place.* Santa Fe: School of American Research.

Fingarette, H. (1988). *Heavy drinking: The myth of alcoholism as a disease.* Berkeley: University of California Press.

Flynn, S. (2000, August). The perfect fire. *Esquire, 134*(1) 64-79, 129, 131-133.

Fornari, F. (1975). *The Psychoanalysis of war.* (A. Pfeifer, Trans.) New York: Doubleday/Anchor. (Original work published in 1966)

Forsyth, D. W. (1999). Proposals regarding the evolution of fatherhood. *Journal for the Psychoanalysis of Culture and Society, 4*,1, 39-49.

Frank, G. (2000). [Review of the book *Healing dramas and clinical plots: The narrative structure of experience*]. *Medical Anthropology Quarterly, 14*(1), 112-113.

Freeman, J. (1999). Note on "Family-L" listserve, on the subject of "Docs as Cops," 6 August. FAMILY-L@LSV.UKY.EDU

Freud, A. (1936). *The ego and the mechanisms of defense.* Madison, CT: International Universities Press.

Freud, S. (1953). The interpretation of dreams. In J. Strachey (Ed. & Trans.), *The standard edition of the complete psychological works of Sigmund Freud*, (Vols. 4-5, pp. 1-627). London: Hogarth Press. (Original work published 1900)

Freud, S. (1958). Recommendations to physicians practicing psycho-analysis. In J. Strachey (Ed. & Trans.), *The standard edition of the complete psychological works of Sigmund Freud* (Vol. 12, pp. 111-120). London: Hogarth Press. (Original work published 1912)

Freud, S. (1958). Remembering, repeating, and working-through. In J. Strachey (Ed. & Trans.), *The standard edition of the complete psychological works of Sigmund Freud* (Vol. 12, pp. 145-156). London: Hogarth Press. (Original work published 1914)

Freud, S. (1957). Mourning and melancholia. In J. Strachey (Ed. & Trans.), *The standard edition of the complete psychological works of Sigmund Freud*, (Vol. 14, pp. 243-258). London: Hogarth Press. (Original work published 1917)

Freud, S. (1955). Beyond the pleasure principle. In J. Strachey (Ed.& Trans.), *The standard edition of the complete psychological works of Sigmund Freud.* (Vol. 18. pp. 7-64). London: Hogarth Press. (Original work published 1920)

Freud, S. (1955). Group psychology and the analysis of the ego. In J. Strachey (Ed. & Trans.), *The standard edition of the complete psychological works of Sigmund Freud.* (Vol. 18, pp. 69-143). London: Hogarth Press. (Original work published 1921)

Freud. S. (1961). Dostoevsky and parricide. In J. Strachey (Ed. & Trans.), *The standard edition of the complete psychological works of Sigmund Freud* (Vol. 21, pp. 177-194). London: Hogarth Press. (Original work published 1928)

Freud, S. (1961). Civilization and its discontents. In J. Strachey (Ed. & Trans.), *The standard edition of the complete psychological workd of Sigmund Freud* (Vol. 21, pp. 64-145). London: Hogarth Press, (Original work published 1930).

Freud S. & Oppenheim, D. E.. (1958). *Dreams in folklore.* New York: International Universities Press. (Original work published 1911)

Fukuyama, F. (1991). *The end of history and the last man.* New York: Free Press.

Fullilove, M. T. (1996). Psychiatric implications of displacement: contributions from the psychology of place. *American Journal of Psychiatry, 153*, 1516-1523.

Gabriel, Y. (2000). *Storytelling in organizations: Facts, fictions, and fantasies.* Oxford: Oxford University Press.

Gadpaille, W. J. (1967). The analyst as auxiliary ego in the treatment of action-disturbed patients. *Science and Psychoanalysis, 11*, 161-181.

Geertz, C. (1983). From the native's point of view: On the nature of anthropological understanding. In *Local knowledge: Further essays in interpretive anthropology* (pp. 55-70). New York: Basic Books.

Gibbs, N. (2001, February 19). Baby it's you! And you, and you.... *Time, 157*, 46-57.

Gibbs, N. & Roche, T. (1999, December 20). The Columbine tapes. *Time, 154*, 40-59.

Gilligan, J. (1997). *Violence: Reflections on a national epidemic.* New York: Vintage.

Glass, J. M. (1999). Two models of political organization: Collaboration versus resistance. *American Behavioral Scientist, 43*,2, 278-3000.

Glover, E. (1933). *War, sadism and pacifism.* London: Allen and Unwin.

Goertzel, T. (2002). In search of Bin Laden. *Clio's Psyche, 8*(4), 178-180.

Goffman, E. (1963). *Stigma: Notes on the management of spoiled identity.* Englewood Cliffs, N.J: Prentice-Hall.

Goodheart, A. (2002). The skyscraper and the airplane. *The American Scholar, 71*(1), 13-19.

Goodman, E. (1999, May 3). Parental-responsibility advocates might have found their poster families. But is it really clear who's at fault? *The Philadelphia Inquirer.* Retrieved July 12, 1999, from (http://phillynews.com/programs/aprint).

Goodman, E. (1999, May 4). Parents sometimes try, but fail. *The Dallas Morning News,* p. 15A.

Goodman, E. (2001, April 4). Clone con job: Grief becomes driving force to duplicate a human being. *The Dallas Morning News,* p. 15A.

Grier, W. H. & Cobbs, P. M. (1992). *Black Rage.* New York: Basic Books.

Group for the Advancement of Psychiatry. Committee on International Relations & H.F. Stein. (1987). *Us and them: The psychology of ethnonationalism.* New York: Brunner/Mazel. (GAP Report No. 123).

Gruen, A. (1999). The need to punish: The political consequences of identifying with the aggressor. *Journal of Psychohistory*, *27*(2), 136-154.

Hallowell, A. I. (1955). *Culture and experience.* Philadelphia: University of Pennsylvania Press.

Hammer, M. (1990, July-August). Reengineering work: Don't automate, obliterate. *Harvard Business Review*, 104-112.

Hammer, M. & J. Champy. (1993). *Reengineering the corporation: A manifesto for business revolution.* New York: HarperCollins.

Heath, D. B. (1989). The new temperance movement: Through the looking-glass. In E. S. Lisansky Gomberg (Guest Ed.), *Current Issues in Alcohol/Drug Studies* (pp. 143-168). *Drugs and Society, 3*,3/4.

Hilberg, R. (1992). *Perpetrators, victims, bystanders: The Jewish catastrophe 1933-1945.* New York: Aaron Asher Books.

Hirsch, I. (1996). Observing participation, mutual enactment, and the new classical models. *Contemporary Psychoanalysis, 332*, 359-383.

Hobsbawm, E. (Ed.). (1983). *The invention of tradition.* Cambridge: Cambridge University Press.

Hughes, J. L. (2000). Avoidance of emotional pain during downsizing in a public agency. *Consulting Psychology Journal: Research and Practice*, *52*(4), 256-268.

Human cloning is closer than you think. (2001, February 17) *TIME,157*, [cover].

Huntington, S. P. (1998). *The clash of civilizations and the remaking of world order.* New York: Touchstone.

Ignatius, D. (2001, October 28) The psyche of a Bin Laden. *The Washington Post*, p. B7.

Immelman, A. (2002). Mohamed Atta's personality. *Clio's Psyche*, *8*(4), 185-189.

Isaacs, H. R. (1989). *Idols of the tribe: Group identity and political change.* Cambridge: Harvard University Press. (Original work published 1975)

Javors, I. (2000). Grief that dares not speak its name. *Clio's Psyche, 7*(2), 88-89.

Kabaphes (Cavafy), K. (1948). *The complete poems of Cavafy.* (R. Dalven, trans.). New York: Harcourt Brace Jovanovich.

Klein, M. (1946). Notes on some schizoid mechanisms. *International Journal of Psycho-Analysis, 27*, 99-110.

Kleinman, A. (1988). *The illness narratives: Suffering, healing and the human condition.* New York: Basic Books.

Kleinman, A., Das, V. & Lock. M. (Eds.) (1997). *Social suffering.* Berkeley: University of California Press.

Kluckhohn, F. R. & Strodtbeck, F. L. (1961). *Variations in value orientations.* Evanston, Illinois: Row Peterson.

Kobrin, N. H. (2002). A psychoanalytic approach to Bin Laden, political violence, and Islamic suicidal terrorism. *Clio's Psyche*, *8*(4), 181-183.

Koenigsberg, R. (1975). *Hitler's ideology: A study in psychoanalytic sociology.* New York: Library of Social Science.

Kohut, H. (1972). Thoughts on narcissism and narcissistic rage. *The psychoanalytic study of the child,* 360-400 (Vol. 27), New York: Quadrangle/The New York Times Press.

Korzybski, A. (1941). *Science and sanity.* New York: Science Press.

Kren, G. M. & Rappoport, L (1994). *The Holocaust and the crisis of human behavior* (Rev. ed.). New York: Holmes and Meier. (Original work published 1980).

Krystal, H. (1988). *Integration and self-healing: Affect, trauma, alexithymia.* Hillsdale, NJ.: Jason Aronson.

Kurth, F. (1975). Projective identification, analyzability, and hate. *Psychoanalytic Forum*, 5, 313-352.

Kurth, W. (2002). Measuring the dynamics of group-fantasy by image analysis. *The Journal of Psychohistory*, *30*(2), 112-129.

La Barre, W. (1946). Social cynosure and social structure. *Journal of Personality,* 14, 169-183.

La Barre, W. (1954). *The human animal.* Chicago: University of Chicago Press.

La Barre, W. (1969). *They shall take up serpents: Psychology of the Southern snake-handling cult.* New York: Schocken.

La Barre, W. (1971). Materials for a history of studies of crisis cults: A bibliographic essay. *Current Anthropology, 12*(1), 3-44.

La Barre, W. (1972). *The Ghost Dance: The origins of religion.* New York: Dell.

Laub, D. & Podell, D. (1997). Psychoanalytic listening to historical trauma: The conflict of knowing and the imperative to act. *Mind and Human Interaction, 8*,4 , 245-260.

Levine, D. P. (1998). Hatred of government. *Administrative Theory and Praxis*, *20*(3), 326-345.

Levine, D. P. (1999). The capacity for ethical conduct. *Psychoanalytic Studies, 1*(1), 73-85.

Levine, D. (2002). Tolerating difference and coping with the infidel. *Journal for the Psychoanalysis of Culture and Society*, *7*(1), 43-53.

Lewis, B. (2001). *What went wrong: Western impact and Middle Eastern response.* Oxford: Oxford University Press.

Lewis, D. L. (2002). In Morocco. *The American Scholar*, *71*(1), 38-40.

Loewenberg, P. (1971, December). The psychohistorical origins of the Nazi youth cohort. *American Historical Review, 76* , 1457-1502.

Lofholm, N. (2000, July 28). Utes see 'spirits' in calamities [fire in Mesa Verde National Park]. *The Denver Post*, pp. 1A, 7A.

Luel S. A. & Marcus, P. (Eds.). (1984). *Psychoanalytic reflections on the Holocaust.* New York: Holocaust Awareness Institute, Center for Judaic Studies, University of Denver; and KTAV Publishing House.

Lukashevich, S. (1968). [Review of the book *Panslavisme et solidarité Slave au XIXe siècle: La Société des Slaves Unis* (1823-1825)] *Slavic and East European Journal*, *12*, 121.

Malefijt, A. de W. (1968). Homo monstrosus. *Scientific American.* 219, 113-118.

Masterson, J. (1983). *Countertransference and psychotherapeutic technique.* New York: Brunner/Mazel.

Mattingly, C. (1998). *Healing dramas and clinical plots: The narrative structure of experience.* Cambridge: Cambridge University Press.

McNally, R. J. (2003). *Remembering trauma.* Cambridge: Harvard University Press.

Mersky, R. R. (1999, June). *Falling from grace, when consultants go out of role: Enactment in the service of the consultation.* Paper presented at the meeting of the International Society for the Psychoanalytic Study of Organizations. 1999 Symposium, Toronto, Ontario, Canada.

Micklethwait, J. & Wooldridge. A. (1996). *The witch doctors: Making sense of the management gurus.* New York: Times Books.

Miller, A. (1983). *For your own good: Hidden cruelty in child-rearing and the roots of violence.* New York: Farrar, Straus & Giroux.

Mitchell, J. T. (1996, March). Critical Incident Stress Debriefing. Material presented at Stress and Trauma Courses, Naval Medical Center, Portsmouth, VA.

Mitchell, J. T. & Everly, G. S., Jr. (1995). *Critical Incident Stress Management: The basic course workbook.* Ellicott City, MD: International Critical Incident Stress Foundation, Inc.

Mitscherlich, A. (1969). *Society without the father: A contribution to social psychology.* New York: Harcourt, Brace and World.

Mitscherlich, A. & Mitscherlich, M. (1975). *The inability to mourn: Principles of collective behavior.* New York: Grove Press, (orig. 1967)

The monsters next door: A special report on the Colorado school massacre (1999, May 3). *TIME. 153,* [cover].

Moses, R. (1990). Acknowledgment: The balm of narcissistic injuries. *Mind and Human Interaction, 2*(2), 28-30.

Muller, H. (1957). *Uses of the Past.* Oxford: Oxford University Press.

Niederland, W. G. (1961). The problem of the survivor. *Journal of Hillside Hospital, 10*, 233-247.

Niederland, W. G. (1964). Psychiatric disorders among persecution victims. *Journal of Nervous and Mental Disorders, 139*, 458-474.

Novak, M. (1971). *The rise of the unmeltable ethnics.* New York: Macmillan.

Novak, M. (1974). The new ethnicity. *The Center Magazine, 7*(4), 18-25.

Ochberg, F. (1988). *Post-traumatic therapy and victims of violence.* New York: Brunner-Routledge.

Ochberg, F. (1997). Introduction: Twenty years after defining PTSD. *Mind and Human Interaction, 8*(4), 201-203.

Ogden, T.H. (1989). *The primitive edge of experience.* Northvale, NJ: Jason Aronson.

Ogden, T.H. (1996). *Subjects of analysis.* Northvale, NJ: Jason Aronson.

Oliver-Smith, A. (1992). *The martyred city: Death and rebirth in the Andes.* Prospect Heights, IL: Waveland Press.

Paul, R. A. (1980). Symbolic interpretation in psychoanalysis and anthropology. *Ethos, 8*, 286-294.

Peters, M. (2001, April 7). *The Dallas Morning News*, p. 31A

Piven, J. S. (2002). Lacanian psychohistory? Or the purloined past. *Psychohistory, Newsletter of the International Psychohistorical Association*, *21*(3), 7-12.

Precker, M. (2001, February 20). Fired out: Undignified layoff techniques can make a bad situation much worse. *The Dallas Morning News*, pp. C-1, C-2.

Proctor, R. (1988). *Racial hygiene: Medicine under the Nazis.* Cambridge, MA: Harvard University Press.

Rando, T. A. (1994). Complications in mourning traumatic death. In I. Corless, B. Germino, & M. Pittman (Eds.), *Dying, death, and bereavement: Theoretical perspectives and other ways of knowing* (pp. 253-271). Boston: Jones and Bartlett Publishers.

Rando, T. A. (1996). On treating those bereaved by sudden, unanticipated death. *In Session: Psychotherapy in Practice*, *2*(4), 59-71.

Rangell, L. (1976). Discussion of the Buffalo Creek disaster: The course of psychic trauma. *American Journal of Psychiatry, 133*, 313-316.

Rao, C.P. (Ed). (1998). *Globalization, privatization and free market economy.* Westport, CT: Quorum Books.

Ritzer, G. (2000). *The McDonaldization of society* (3rd ed). Thousand Oaks, CA: Sage Publications.

Roberts, C. & Roberts, S. (2002, March 9). Selling America to Muslims is tough: A religious barrier has replaced the Iron Curtain. *The Dallas Morning News*, p. 27A.

Rochlin, G. (1973). *Man's aggression: The defense of the self.* Boston: Gambit.

Rotella, C. (2002). Affliction. *The American Scholar, 71*(1), 48-51.

Rowlands, M. (1998). Trauma, memory and memorials. *British Journal of Psychotherapy, 15*(1), 54-64.

Russakoff, D., Goldstein, A. & Achenbach, J. (1999, May 2). Shooters' neighbors had little hint. *The Washington Post,* p. A1.

Shatan, C. F. (1997). Living in a split time zone: Trauma and therapy of Vietnam combat survivors. *Mind and Human Interaction*, *8*(4), 204-222.

Sievers, B. (1995). *Work, death, and life itself: Essays on management and organization*. New York and Berlin: Walter de Gruyter.

Silver, R. C., Holman, E. A., McIntosh, D. N., Poulin, M., & V. Gil-Rivas. (2002). Nationwide longitudinal study of psychological responses to September 11. *Journal of the American Medical Association*, *288*(10)September 11, 1235-1244.

Spence, D. (1982). *Narrative truth and historical truth*. New York: Norton.

Spicer, E. H. (1971). Persistent cultural systems. *Science, 1174*, 795-800.

Spiegelman, A. (2001). Retrieved June 14, 2001 from (http://dailynews.yahoo.com,/h/nm/20010611/ts/mcveigh_leadall_dc_dc_27.html).

Spiro, M. E. (1986). Cultural relativism and the future of anthropology. *Cultural Anthropology 1*, 259-286.

Spiro, M.E. (2001). Cultural determinism, cultural relativism, and the comparative study of psychopathology. *Ethos*, *29*(2), 218-234.

Stein, H. F. (1976). Russian nationalism and the divided soul of the Westernizers and Slavophiles. *Ethos*, *4*(4),403-438.

Stein, H. F. (1978). Aging and death among Slovak-Americans: A study in the thematic unity of the life cycle. *Journal of Psychological Anthropology, 1*(3), 297-320.

Stein, H. F. (1982a). Adversary symbiosis and complementary group dissociation: An analysis of the U.S./U.S.S.R. conflict. *International Journal of Intercultural Relations*, *6*, 55-83.

Stein, H. F. (1982b). Ethanol and Its discontents: Paradoxes of inebriation and sobriety in American culture. *The Journal of Psychoanalytic Anthropology, 5*(4), 355-377.

Stein, H. F. (1985). Alcoholism as metaphor in American culture: Ritual desecration as social integration. *Ethos, 13*(3), 195-235.

Stein, H. F. (1987). *Developmental time, cultural space: Studies in psychogeography*. Norman, OK: University of Oklahoma Press.

Stein, H. F. (1990a). In what systems do alcohol/chemical addictions make sense?: Clinical ideologies and practices as cultural metaphors. *Social Science and Medicine, 30*,*9*, 987-1000.

Stein, H. F. (1990b). The internal and group milieux of ethnicity: Identifying generic group psychodynamic issues. *Canadian Review of Studies in Nationalism,* 17(1-2), 107-130.

Stein, H. F. (1993a). *The culture of Oklahoma*. Norman, OK: University of Oklahoma Press.

Stein, H.F. (1993b). Substance and symbol. In M. Galanter, (Ed.), *Recent developments in alcoholism, Volume 11: Ten Years of Progress* (pp. 153-164). New York: Plenum.

Stein, H. F. (1994a). *Listening deeply*. Boulder: Westview Press.

Stein, H. F. (1994b). *The dream of culture*. New York: Psyche Press.

Stein, H. F. (1995). Reflections on the Oklahoma City bombing: War, mourning, and the brief mercies of plenty. *Mind and Human Interaction*, *6*(4), 186-199.

Stein, H. F. (1996a). *Prairie voices: Process anthropology in family medicine*. Westport, CT: Bergin & Garvey.

Stein, H.F. (1996b). Oklahoma City aftermath: Trauma, time, and adaptation—A psychohistorical montage. *Clio's Psyche*, *2*(4), 92-95.

Stein, H. F. (1997a). Disaster, community, culture, and the practice of Anthropology: Some reflections and lessons from the Oklahoma City Bombing. *High Plains Applied Anthropologist*, *17*(1), Spring, 69-82.

Stein, H. F. (1997b). Trauma revisited: Mourning and the unconscious in the Oklahoma City bombing. *Journal for the Psychoanalysis of Culture and Society, 2*(1), 17-37.

Stein, H. F. (1998a). *Euphemism, spin, and the crisis in organizational life.* Westport, CT: Quorum Books.

Stein, H. F. (1998b). Organizational euphemism and the cultural mystification of evil. *Administrative Theory and Praxis, 20*(3), 346-357.

Stein, H. F. (1999a). Downsizing, managed care, and the potlatching of America: A study in cultural brutality and its mystification. *Journal for the Psychoanalysis of Culture and Society, 4*,(2) 209-227.

Stein, H. F. (1999b). A bombing in April: Culture and disaster in the Oklahoma City bombing. *Illness, Crisis and Loss*, *7*(1), 17-36.

Stein, H. F. (2000). From countertransference to social theory: A study of Holocaust thinking in U.S. business dress. *Ethos*, *28*(3), 346-378.

Stein, H. F. (2001a). *Nothing personal, just business: A guided journey into organizational darkness.* Westport, CT: Quorum Books.

Stein, H. F. (2001b). The left out and the forgotten: Notes on the emics and etics of disasters. *High Plains Applied Anthropologist*, *21*(1), 1-24.

Stein, H. F. (2001c). Mourning and society: A study in the history and philosophy of science, *Mind and Human Interaction*, *12*(2), 82-94.

Stein, H. F. & Apprey, M. (1987). *From metaphor to meaning: Papers in psychoanalytic anthropology.* Charlottesville, VA: University Press of Virginia.

Stein, H. F. & Apprey, M. (1990). *Clinical stories and their translations.* Charlottesville, VA: University Press of Virginia.

Stein, H. F. & Hill, R. F. (1977). *The ethnic imperative: Exploring the new White Ethnic movement.* University Park, PA: Pennsylvania State University Press.

Stein, H. F. & Hill, R. F. (1988). The dogma of technology. In L. B. Boyer, S. Grolnick (Eds.), *The Psychoanalytic Study of Society*, *Vol. 13_* (pp. 149-179). Hillsdale, NJ: The Analytic Press.

Stein, H. F. & Niederland, W. F., (Eds.). *Maps from the mind: Readings in psychogeography.* Norman: University of Oklahoma Press.

Stickney, B. M. (1996). *All-American monster: The unauthorized biography of Timothy McVeigh.* Amherst, NY: Prometheus Books.

Streeck-Fischer, A. (1999). Naziskins in Germany: Traumatization in the past and the present. *Mind and Human Interaction*, *10*(2), 20-33.

Suarez-Orozco, M. M. (1990). Speaking of the unspeakable: Toward a psychosocial understanding of responses to terror. *Ethos, 18*(3), 353-383.

Taylor, F. W. (1911). *Principles of scientific management.* New York: Harper.

Taylor, S. E. (1983). Adjustment to threatening events: A theory of cognitive adaptation. *American Psychologist, 38*(11), 1161-1173.

Terry, J. (1984). The damaging effects of the 'Survivor Syndrome.' In S.A. Luel & P. Marcus (Eds.), *Psychoanalytic reflections on the Holocaust* (pp. 135-148). New York: Holocaust Awareness Institute, Center for Judaic Studies, University of Denver, & KTAV Publishing House.

Tramel, B. W. (1993). The significance of sports in Oklahoma. In H. F. Stein & R. F. Hill (Eds.), *The culture of Oklahoma* (pp. 143-159). Norman, OK: University of Oklahoma Press.

Turner, V. (1970). *Forest of symbols: Aspects of Ndembu rituals.* Ithaca, NY: Cornell University Press.

Vaughan, K. (1999, October 16). Klebold family plans to sue Jeffco. Denver Rocky Mountain News.

Vekilovsky, I. (1950). *Worlds in Collision.* New York: Dell.

Vognar, C. (2002, March 3). Hollywood marches back to war. *The Dallas Morning News*, pp. 1J, 6J.

Volkan, V. D. (1981). *Linking objects and linking phenomena.* New York: International Universities Press.

Volkan, V. D. (1988). *The need to have enemies and allies: From clinical practice to international relationships.* Northvale, NJ: Jason Aronson.

Volkan, V. D. (1991). On 'chosen' trauma. *Mind and Human Interaction, 3*(1), July, 13.

Volkan, V. D. (1997). *Blood Lines: From ethnic pride to ethnic terrorism.* Boulder, CO: Westview Press..

Volkan, V. D. (2000). Traumatized societies and psychological care: Expanding the concept of preventive medicine. *Mind and Human Interaction, 11*(3), 177-194.

White, J.B. (1996, November 26). 'Next best thing': Reengineering gurus take steps to remodel their stalling vehicles. *The Wall Street Journal*, pp. A1, 13.

Whitehead, A. N. (1925). *Science and the modern world.* New York: Macmillan.

Winnicott, D. W. (1958). *Collected papers.* London: Tavistock.

Winnicott, D.W. (1965). *The maturational processes and the facilitating environment.* New York: International Universities Press.

Wynne, L. (1965). Some indications and contraindications for exploratory family therapy. In I. Boszormenyi-Nagy & J. L. Framo (Eds.), *Intensive family therapy: Theoretical and practical aspects* (pp. 289-322). New York: Harper and Row.

Young, A. (1995). *The harmony of illusions: Inventing post-traumatic stress disorder.* Princeton: Princeton University Press.

Zimmerman, J. (1999, October 25). Criticizing cult of high school sports. *The Oklahoma Observer*, p. 13.

Index